ASVAB WORD KNOWLEDGE WORKBOOK

Review of ASVAB Vocabulary and Word Knowledge Practice Tests for the ASVAB Test and AFQT

The ASVAB is a registered trademark by the United States Department of Defense, which is not affiliated with nor endorses this publication.

ASVAB Word Knowledge Workbook: Review of ASVAB Vocabulary and Word Knowledge Practice Tests for the ASVAB Test and AFQT

© COPYRIGHT 2016

Exam SAM Study Aids & Media dba www.examsam.com

All rights reserved. No part of this publication may be reproduced, stored in a retrieval system, or transmitted, in any form or by any means, electronic, mechanical, photocopying, recording, or otherwise, without the prior written permission of the copyright owner.

ISBN-13: 978-1-949282-12-2
ISBN-10: 1-949282-12-0

For information on bulk discounts, please contact us at: email@examsam.com

NOTE: The ASVAB and AFQT are registered trademarks of the United States Department of Defense, which is not affiliated with nor endorses this publication.

ABBREVIATIONS USED IN THIS PUBLICATION

adj.	adjective
adv.	adverb
ant.	antonym
e.g.	example
esp.	especially
met.	metaphorical
n.	noun
pl.	plural
sbdy	somebody
sthg	something
syn.	synonym.
verb	v.

FURTHER ASVAB PRACTICE

In order to do your best on the day of your test, you may also like to consider our other publications:

ASVAB Study Guide - Reading Skills: Reading Skill Preparation & Strategies and Paragraph Comprehension Practice Tests for the ASVAB Test and AFQT

ASVAB Arithmetic Reasoning Practice Tests: ASVAB Arithmetic Study Guide and Arithmetic Reasoning Practice Tests for the ASVAB Test and AFQT

ASVAB Practice Test Book - Mathematics Knowledge: ASVAB Math Study Guide and Mathematics Knowledge Practice Tests for the ASVAB Test and AFQT

TABLE OF CONTENTS

Words beginning with "A" – Definitions and example sentences	1
Words beginning with "A" – Exercises	7
Words beginning with "B" – Definitions and example sentences	8
Words beginning with "B" – Exercises	11
Words beginning with "C" – Definitions and example sentences	12
Words beginning with "C" – Exercises	19
Words beginning with "D" – Definitions and example sentences	20
Words beginning with "D" – Exercises	26
Words beginning with "E" – Definitions and example sentences	27
Words beginning with "E" – Exercises	32
Words beginning with "F" – Definitions and example sentences	33
Words beginning with "F" – Exercises	37
Words beginning "G – H" – Definitions and example sentences	38
Words beginning with "G – H" – Exercises	41
Words beginning with "I" – Definitions and example sentences	42
Words beginning with "I" – Exercises	48
Words beginning "J – L" – Definitions and example sentences	49
Words beginning "J – L" – Exercises	52
Words beginning "M – O" – Definitions and example sentences	53
Words beginning "M – O" – Exercises	57
Words beginning with "P" – Definitions and example sentences	58
Words beginning with "P" – Exercises	63
Words beginning "Q – R" – Definitions and example sentences	64

Words beginning "Q – R" – Exercises	69
Words beginning with "S" – Definitions and example sentences	70
Words beginning with "S" – Exercises	77
Words beginning with "T" – Definitions and example sentences	78
Words beginning with "T" – Exercises	81
Words beginning "U – V" – Definitions and example sentences	82
Words beginning "U - V" – Exercises	86
Words beginning "W – Z" – Definitions and example sentences	87
Words beginning "W – Z" – Exercises	89
ASVAB AFQT Word Knowledge Practice Test 1	90
ASVAB AFQT Word Knowledge Practice Test 2	93
ASVAB AFQT Word Knowledge Practice Test 3	96
ASVAB AFQT Word Knowledge Practice Test 4	99
ASVAB AFQT Word Knowledge Practice Test 5	102
ASVAB AFQT Word Knowledge Practice Test 6	105
ASVAB AFQT Word Knowledge Practice Test 7	108
ASVAB AFQT Word Knowledge Practice Test 8	111
Answers to the Exercises	114
Answers to the Practice Tests	122
Appendix 1 – ASVAB and AFQT Test Information	130
Appendix 2 – How to use this publication	131
Appendix 3 – Information for Educators	132

Words – A

Instructions: Study the words below, paying attention to their meanings as well as how they are used in the example sentences. Then complete the exercise that follows.

abate	(v.) to lessen in intensity or amount. e.g. - The county has decided to abate real estate taxes for families with more than three children in school this year.
abdicate	(v.) to relinquish political, royal, or regal power to someone else. e.g. - King Edward abdicated his right to the throne to marry his true love and live as a commoner. (n.) abdication.
abeyance	(n.) the act of temporarily stopping a problem or issue. e.g. - We don't need to consider that issue, so let's hold it in abeyance for now. (adj.) abeyant.
abhorrent	(adj.) terrible, causing intense conflict or hatred. e.g. - Cheating and lying are abhorrent behaviors. (n.) abhorrence; (v.) abhor; (adj.) abhorrently.
abound	(v.) to be present in large amounts or quantities; to be prevalent. e.g. - There are more than one hundred items on the menu at that restaurant, so your choices abound.
abridge	(v.) shorten. e.g. - You will need to abridge that document as it is too long now.
abrogate	(v.) to abolish or annul officially; to treat sthg as if it doesn't exist. e.g. - That old law has been abrogated since a new law has been created to address the problem.
abscond	(v.) to leave a place secretly and go into hiding with stolen money. e.g. - Jeff stole money from the company for which he was chief accountant. Later, he absconded with the funds and is currently thought to be living in Brazil. (adj.) absconded.
abyss	(n.) a gap between two cliffs; (syn.) chasm. e.g. - He fell into the abyss while mountain climbing. (adj.) abysmal.
accord	(n.) agreement. e.g. - We are in accord about this solution, so there is no need for further discussion. (n.) accordance; (v.) accord.
accost	(v.) to attack; to confront aggressively. e.g. - He was accosted by an attacker in the street and was badly injured.

accumulate	(v.) to increase gradually in amount or quantity. e.g. - She did not become a millionaire overnight. She <u>accumulated</u> her wealth over many years. (n.) accumulation; (adj.) accumulative; (adv.) accumulatively.
accustomed (to)	(adj.) having become familiar with or used to certain conditions because of habit or experience. e.g. - I became <u>accustomed</u> to getting up early after having had a class at 8:00 this semester. (v.) accustom.
acquit	(v.) to find an accused suspect not guilty of a crime in court. e.g. - The suspect was <u>acquitted</u> of the crime when he was found "not guilty" by the court. (n.) acquittal.
acrimony	(n.) bitterness, disharmony, or hatred. e.g. - That couple is arguing in public all the time, so their <u>acrimony</u> for each other is easy to see. (adj.) acrimonious.
acquiesce	(v.) to accept sthg reluctantly. e.g. - The police <u>acquiesced</u> to the proposal when no acceptable alternative could be found. (n.) acquiescence; (adj.) acquiesced.
acrid	(adj.) having a strong or bitter smell. e.g. - The field was filled with <u>acrid</u> smoke after the gunfire.
acuity	(n.) sharpness or precision. e.g. - His intellectual <u>acuity</u> is indisputable as he has a degree from Harvard.
acute	(adj.) sharp; in very serious condition. e.g. - She had an <u>acute</u> pain in her stomach and was rushed to the hospital.
adage	(n.) an expression, saying, or proverb. e.g. - My favorite <u>adage</u> is: Don't count your chickens before they are hatched.
adept	(adj.) displaying great skill or talent for sthg. e.g. - He is very <u>adept</u> at art. In fact, his paintings have been displayed in the most famous museums in New York. (ant.) inept.
adjacent	(adj.) being next door or nearby. e.g. - You don't need to go far to buy bread. There is a grocery store <u>adjacent</u> to our house. (n.) adjacency.
adjourn	(v.) to dismiss a meeting or call it to a close. e.g. - The business meeting began at 12:00 and was <u>adjourned</u> at 2:00.
advent (of)	(n.) arrival; coming into use or existence. e.g. - The <u>advent</u> of the new computer system means that the old system will be disposed of.
adversary	(n.) enemy, opponent, or antagonist. e.g. - The boxer hit his <u>adversary</u> with great strength. (n.) adversity; (adj.) adversarial.

adverse	(adj.) negative or in opposition to the interests of. e.g. - <u>Adverse</u> weather conditions made travel out of the question. (n.) adversity; (adv.) adversely.
advocate	(n.) defender or supporter of a specific cause or issue; (syn.) proponent. e.g. - He is an <u>advocate</u> of that political party since he supports their policies. (v.) advocate.
affable	(adj.) pleasant; friendly; (syn.) winsome, amiable, cordial. e.g. - James is an <u>affable</u> fellow and is pleasant company. (n.) affability; (adv.) affably.
affiliation	(n.) an association or close relationship of members of a group; (syn.) alliance. e.g. - Many large American companies are actually an <u>affiliation</u> of several smaller companies. (v.) affiliate.
affirm	(v.) to promise or declare positively. e.g. - I <u>affirm</u> that I will provide my assistance in the matter. You can depend on me. (n.) affirmation.
afflict (with)	(v.) to cause pain or suffering. e.g. - She has been <u>afflicted</u> with cancer and is currently undergoing therapy. (n.) affliction.
affluent	(adj.) rich; wealthy; well-to-do; well-off. e.g. - Alan is from an <u>affluent</u> family. They own five cars, three houses, and a yacht. (n.) affluence; (adv.) affluently.
aghast	(adj.) shocked or appalled. e.g. - He was <u>aghast</u> when he was told that his house had burned to the ground.
ailment	(n.) an illness or disease. e.g. - He is suffering from a strange <u>ailment</u> and has been in bed for three weeks. (v.) ail; (adj.) ailing.
alacrity	(n.) the willingness or readiness to carry out a specific action. e.g. - Sarah is an eager student and studies with <u>alacrity</u>.
alliance	(n.) co-operation of allies or members; (syn.) affiliation. e.g. - The United Kingdom and the United States often form <u>alliances</u>, especially during times of war. (adj.) allied.
allocate	(v.) to set aside in shares. e.g. - The profit was evenly <u>allocated</u> among all of the partners of the company. (n.) allocation; (adj.) allocated.
allot	(v.) to allocate or distribute in shares. e.g. - The father had a dozen cookies and <u>allotted</u> four of them to each of his three children. (n.) allotment; (adj.) allotted.
allude (to)	(v.) to imply by inference or indirect speech. e.g. - He <u>alluded</u> to the idea that I had become fat by asking if I was wearing a larger dress size now. (n.) allusion.

aloof	(adj.) reserved or indifferent to the interests or feelings of others. e.g. - Bryce is so aloof that he often avoids our company. (n.) aloofness; (adv.) aloofly.
altruistic	(adj.) relating to concern for the well-being of others. e.g. - He is one of the most altruistic men in the city as he constantly gives money to the poor. (n.) altruism.
amateur	(n.) a person who is not professional; a person who does not display skill or expertise in a given subject. e.g. - Their wedding photographer was clearly an amateur as all of their photographs turned out to be blurry. (adj.) amateur; amateurish.
ambiance	(n.) atmosphere; surroundings. e.g. - The ambiance at the party was very cheerful. Everyone was in a great mood. (adj.) ambient.
ambiguous	(adj.) unclear in meaning. e.g. - The professor's instructions were so ambiguous that none of the students could understand them. (n.) ambiguity; (adv.) ambiguously.
amiable	(adj.) pleasant; friendly; (syn.) affable, winsome, cordial. e.g. - Pam has an amiable personality and makes friends easily. (adv.) amiably.
amiss	(adv.) wrong; mistaken. e.g. - I hope you won't take it amiss if I ask whether you have gained weight.
amity	(n.) love or friendship; (syn.) accord. e.g. - There has been amity between the two nations since they signed the peace treaty. (adj.) amicable.
animosity	(n.) feelings of hostility which can result in aggression. e.g. - Bob felt great animosity towards his boss for being unfairly fired.
annihilate	(v.) to completely destroy; (syn.) obliterate. e.g. - The village was annihilated as a result of the bombing. (n.) annihilation; (adj.) annihilated.
anomie	(n.) a breakdown in social values or norms. e.g. - There has been anomie in the refugee camp. Because of the desperation of the refugees, it seems that the usual social norms do not exist there. Note: also spelled "anomy."
antagonist	(n.) a person who opposes sthg; (syn.) adversary. e.g. - He is the chief antagonist against the decision. He has been against it from the start. (v.) antagonize; (adj.) antagonistic.
antecedent	(adj.) relating to a preceding or previous event or circumstance. e.g. - A series of negotiations were antecedent to reaching a final agreement. (n.) antecedent.

antipathy	(n.) hatred. e.g. - He expressed great antipathy for the man that killed his brother.
apathetic	(adj.) the state of indifference or lack of enthusiasm. e.g. - We thought he would be excited about going abroad, but he appeared to be totally apathetic about it. (n.) apathy; (adv.) apathetically.
apex	(n.) the highest or best point. e.g. - That company operates at the apex of their industry. That's why they have so many customers.
appalling	(adj.) causing shock or disbelief; (syn.) atrocious. e.g. - John's performance on the exam was appalling. (v.) appall.
apparel	(n.) clothing; garments. e.g. - The department store sells all kinds of clothing, including men's, women's, and children's apparel.
appease	(v.) to calm or subdue. e.g. - We bought the whining children ice cream in an attempt to appease them. (n.) appeasement; (adj.) appeasing.
appellation	(n.) a name or title. e.g. - Her appellation was the Queen of Sheba.
apposite	(adj.) appropriate or suitable under the circumstances. e.g. - Louise is in the hospital, so I think that sending her some flowers would be an apposite gesture. (adv.) appositely.
apprehend	(v.) to capture a criminal who has escaped from the law. e.g. - The prisoner escaped while being transported, but was apprehended three days later. (n.) apprehension; (adj.) apprehensible.
apprehension	(n.) fear caused by uncertainty. e.g.- Sally has a lot of apprehension about starting her new job. She's a nervous wreck. (v.) apprehend; (adj.) apprehensive.
arbiter	(n.) a judge or person who decides the outcome of sthg. e.g. - He has been declared as the arbiter in the dispute between the two companies. (n.) arbitration; (v.) arbitrate.
arbor	(n.) a leafy, shaded area formed by tree branches or vines. e.g. - The couple was sitting in a secluded area in the arbor.
arcanum	(n.) a secret or mystery of nature. e.g. - Witch doctors were believed to cure ill people by using an arcanum. (pl.) arcana.
ardent	(adj.) especially passionate, loving, or devoted. e.g. - They are an ardent couple. I don't think anything could separate them. (adv.) ardently.

arduous	(adj.) exceptionally difficult or demanding. e.g. - The expedition to the North Pole was <u>arduous</u> and left the explorers exhausted. (adv.) arduously.
artifact	(n.) an object or relic of historical significance. e.g. - The archeologists found many <u>artifacts</u> during their dig.
assimilate	(v.) to become part of the mainstream of sthg; to come into conformity. e.g. - Although they were born in Samoa, they seem to have <u>assimilated</u> into American culture since they have lived in the United States for two decades. (n.) assimilation; (adj.) assimilated.
augment	(v.) to make sthg greater or better. e.g. - Studying more will certainly <u>augment</u> your grades. (n.) augmentation; (adj.) augmented.
averse	(adj.) opposed to sthg. e.g. She will not invest in the stock market as she is <u>averse</u> to taking the risk.
avid	(adj.) eager; enthusiastic. e.g. - He is an <u>avid</u> reader and reads three books a week. (n.) avidity, avidness; (adv.) avidly.
avocation	(n.) a hobby or pursuit. e.g. - His <u>avocation</u> is collecting stamps. He does it just because he enjoys it.
avow	(v.) to swear or promise sthg legally or officially. e.g. - The President <u>avowed</u> to uphold the laws of the United States during his inauguration ceremony.

Exercises – A

Instructions: Complete the sentences below, using one of the words beginning with the letter "A" from the previous section. Note that some gaps may have more than one possible answer. You may also need to change the form of the word. The answers are provided at the end of book.

1) The _____ of the hospital with the health insurance company has been an astute business venture.

2) He is an _____ fellow and has a lot of friends.

3) There was a great deal of _____ between the two families because of a long-standing dispute.

4) The final exam is going to be _____, so you had better be well prepared.

5) If you carry out the task with _____ you will finish more quickly.

6) Our teacher made some _____ remarks about how we needed to study harder for our exams.

7) The two teams were _____, and there was a great deal of rivalry between them.

8) That law has been _____ because it was so out-of-date.

9) She _____ to the idea that he was lying by saying that his story was difficult to believe.

10) The _____ at the restaurant was so romantic with its candlelight and music.

Words – B

Instructions: Study the words below, paying attention to their meanings as well as how they are used in the example sentences. Then complete the exercise that follows.

babble	(v.) to talk quickly or incoherently. e.g. - Roseanne was babbling so fast about the accident that no one could understand her. (n.) babble.
baffle	(v.) to confuse or stupefy. e.g. - I can't understand this math homework. It completely baffles me.
banish	(v.) to drive out or force to leave. e.g. - You are banished from this club forever. Don't even try to come back here again. (n.) banishment.
banner	(n.) a large piece of cloth bearing a message or national symbol; (syn.) ensign. e.g. - The fans displayed a message on a banner encouraging their team.
bar	(v.) to ban, exclude, or impede. e.g. - He was barred from the library because he kept causing a disruption when he went there. (adj.) barred.
barrage	(n.) a continuous military bombardment. (met.) an unrelenting, continuous flow of sthg; an onslaught. e.g. - They asked the politician a barrage of questions that she didn't have time to answer.
barrier	(n.) sthg that inhibits or prevents progress or movement; (syn.) stumbling block, hindrance, obstacle. e.g. - A barrier was placed at the end of the street to prevent cars from entering.
beckon	(v.) to call forward. e.g. - The teacher is beckoning you to come forward to the board.
belittle	(v.) to cause to feel inferior. e.g. - Sam always belittles his wife by telling her how stupid she is. Actually, she is quite intelligent.
benison	(n.) a benediction or blessing. e.g. - The minister said a benison at the end of the worship service.
bequest	(n.) the action of leaving money or specific property to another person upon an individual's death. e.g. - A bequest in my uncle's will specifically states that I shall receive $10,000 when he dies. (v.) bequeath.
beset	(v.) to cause trouble or difficulties. e.g. - Tina has been beset with difficulties all her life.

bland	(adj.) tasteless or lacking in flavor; (syn.) insipid. e.g. - These potatoes are bland. I think they could use some salt. (n.) blandness; (adv.) blandly.
blandishment	(n.) compliment. e.g. - Mike gave me a nice blandishment yesterday. He told me that I was the most beautiful girl he'd ever seen. (v.) blandish.
blatant	(adj.) obvious, flagrant, or offensive. e.g. - There is no way that the judge will pardon her after such a blatant offense. (n.) blatancy; (adv.) blatantly.
bleak	(adj.) hopeless; depressing. e.g. - What bleak weather! Gray sky and rain get me down. (n.) bleakness; (adv.) bleakly.
bliss	(n.) a state of extreme happiness. e.g. - Staying in such a wonderful hotel in Paris was pure bliss.
blunder	(n.) error; mistake. e.g. - The accident resulted from his blunder in failing to signal his turn.
blunt	(adj.) not sharp; dull. e.g. - The victim was struck with a blunt object, such as a flat rock or brick. (adv.) bluntly.
boggy	(adj.) muddy, waterlogged, or swamped. e.g. - We marched over the boggy terrain in our boots.
bogus	(adj.) not authentic; fake; (syn.) phony. e.g. - The bogus painting of the "Mona Lisa" is often mistaken for the genuine one.
boisterous	(adj.) extremely loud or noisy. e.g. – The children were being boisterous, so we had to tell them to quieten down.
bolster	(v.) to raise or increase by supporting the cause or interest of sthg. e.g. - Going to Disneyland bolstered the spirits of the terminally-ill children.
boom	(v.) to experience great success or expansion; prosper. e.g. - The college is building new classrooms because enrollment is booming. (n.) boom.
bore	(v.) to dig, esp. with heavy machinery. e.g. - The engineers plan to bore for oil in western Texas.
bountiful	(adj.) existing in great quantity or variety. e.g. - That supermarket has a bountiful selection of different types of food. (n.) bounty; (adv.) bountifully.
breach	(v.) to break or violate the law. e.g. - If you park in a prohibited area, you will breach the law. (n.) breach.
breed	(n.) class, kind, or type. e.g. - The zoo displayed numerous breeds of animals. (v.) breed.

brevity	(n.) the state of being brief or short in time or duration. e.g. - The report was known for its brevity since it was only two pages long. (adj.) brief.
brittle	(adj.) to be prone to breaking or splitting. e.g. - The paper was very brittle, so we were told not to touch it since it might break. (n.) brittleness.
brusque	(adj.) terse or abrupt to the point of being rude or impolite. e.g. - He was very brusque in his response to the grieving family. In fact, he only said a couple of words and them dismissed them. (n.) brusqueness; (adv.) brusquely.
budge	(v.) to move sthg with difficulty. e.g. - Alan tried to move the heavy cabinet, but it wouldn't budge.
buffoon	(n.) a fool or idiot. e.g. - He behaved like a clown during the ceremony, so I am sure that most people will consider him to be a buffoon. (adj.) buffoonish.
bullock	(n.) a small or young bull. e.g. - Although that bullock is small now, it will grow up to be a big bull.
bulwark	(n.) defense or protection against danger. (met.) sthg that gives support or encouragement. e.g. - Religion was his bulwark when he lost his job. He found a great deal of comfort in it. (v.) bulwark.
buoy	(n.) a floating object that indicates a dangerous area in a waterway. e.g. - Don't swim beyond the red and white buoys floating in the water. It's too deep to swim out there. (n.) buoyancy; (adj.) buoyant; (adv.) buoyantly.
burnished	(adj.) polished. e.g. - The burnished copper shone brightly under the light. (v.) burnish.
bureaucratic	(adj.) relating to the administration of the government. e.g. - I had a lot of bureaucratic hassle at the court house this morning when I went to re-new my driver's license. (n.) bureaucracy.
bustle	(v.) to move hurriedly, esp. in order to prepare sthg. e.g. - She had to bustle around this morning. She overslept and was late for work.

Exercises – B

Instructions: Complete the sentences below, using one of the words beginning with the letter "B" from the previous section. Note that some gaps may have more than one possible answer. You may also need to change the form of the word. The answers are provided at the end of book.

1) The crowd at the football game was really loud. In fact, they were _____ .

2) Forts were used as _____ in battle a couple of centuries ago.

3) You will _____ your rental agreement if you leave without paying twelve months' rent.

4) The ship entered the prohibited zone, even though there were _____ demarcating the area.

5) He is always clowning around and acting like a _____ .

6) Her food is always so _____ since she refuses to use any spice or seasoning.

7) She _____ her husband with constant insults. I don't know how he puts up with it.

8) The last section of the exam _____ me. I doubt if I got a single question correct.

9) Telling me I was beautiful and intelligent was such a nice _____.

10) He is so _____ that he never even says good morning.

Words – C

Instructions: Study the words below, paying attention to their meanings as well as how they are used in the example sentences. Then complete the exercise that follows.

cagey	(adj.) relating to the use of cleverness and dishonesty. e.g. - The cagey criminal robbed me after visiting my home under the pretense of being an insurance salesperson.
cajole	(v.) to coax or encourage strongly. e.g. - He cajoled us into joining him for the road trip, although we really didn't want to go. (n.) cajolement.
calamity	(n.) disaster; catastrophe. e.g. - The San Francisco earthquake was one of America's worst natural calamities. (adj.) calamitous.
caliber	(n.) the degree of the capacity or quality of sthg. e.g. - The company has had over one hundred applications for the job, so they will hire someone only of the highest caliber.
candor	(n.) honesty; frankness. e.g. - If I can speak with candor, I must tell you that your behavior is entirely unacceptable. (adj.) candid; (adv.) candidly.
canny	(adj.) displaying good judgement; shrewd. e.g. - The canny shoppers arrived at the store early to get the bargains. (n.) canniness; (adv.) cannily.
capitulate	(v.) to give up or surrender in battle. e.g. - The army capitulated after the enemy's heavy attack. (n.) capitulation.
capsize	(v.) to overturn a boat in a waterway. e.g. - The passenger fell overboard into the water when the boat capsized.
carcass	(n.) the body of a dead animal. e.g. - The carcass of a dead dog, which had been hit by a car, was lying in the center of the road.
carnivorous	(adj.) relating to animals that consume meat. e.g. - Animals such as dogs are carnivorous. They do not eat grass, but rather eat meat. (n.) carnivore.
carouse	(v.) to engage in rowdy or inappropriate behavior, esp. after having consumed too much alcohol. e.g. - Recruits can be discharged if they are repeatedly found to be carousing in public.
castigate	(v.) to punish or reprimand severely. e.g. - The children will be castigated for lying about stealing the candy. (n.) castigation.

caustic	(adj.) relating to sthg that can burn or destroy human tissue. e.g. - That is a <u>caustic</u> chemical, so be sure to wear gloves when you are using it.
censure	(v.) to experience public criticism by one's colleagues. e.g. - The lawyer was <u>censured</u> by the state legal committee for attempting to steal money from a client. (n.) censure.
chagrin	(n.) severe embarrassment or humiliation. e.g. - I felt so <u>chagrined</u> when I realized I was rejected for the job. (adj.) chagrined.
champion	(v.) to support a cause or campaign strongly. e.g. - He <u>championed</u> the abolition of the death penalty.
chasm	(n.) a deep gap in sthg, usually in the surface of the earth; a canyon or gorge. e.g. - There is a bridge over the <u>chasm</u> between the two cliffs.
chide	(v.) to scold or tell off. e.g. - The principal <u>chided</u> the children for their bad behavior.
chimera	(n.) a horrible creature from the imagination; (met.) an impractical or illusory goal. e.g. - After months of searching for a new house without success, the couple feared that their dream home was a <u>chimera</u>.
cite	(v.) to refer to or state. e.g. - The police officer <u>cited</u> the Miranda rights when he arrested the suspect. (n.) citation; (adj.) cited.
clandestine	(adj.) being done or carried out in secrecy. e.g. - The <u>clandestine</u> government operation was known only to a select group of politicians. (adv.) clandestinely.
clarify	(v.) to make clear in meaning. e.g. - The teacher explained the homework again in order to <u>clarify</u> the instructions. (n.) clarity, clarification.
clemency	(n.) the act of giving someone less harsh treatment or of showing mercy or lenience. e.g. - The governor decided to show <u>clemency</u> to the prisoners on death row, and commuted all of their sentences to life in prison. (adj.) clement.
coax	(v.) to influence, persuade, or manipulate; (syn.) cajole. e.g. - Christine was not in the mood to go to the party, but we <u>coaxed</u> her into going by saying that her boyfriend would be there.
cog	(n.) a small tooth-like piece on a wheel-shaped gear. e.g. - The clock was not working because a small <u>cog</u> on the inside had broken off.

cogent	(adj.) logical and credible. e.g. - Saying that the earth is flat is hardly a cogent statement. (adv.) cogently.
cognizant	(adj.) having knowledge or awareness of sthg. e.g. - Politicians should be cognizant of governmental policies and procedures. (n.) cognizance.
coherent	(adj.) easy to understand; logical and consistent. e.g. - He was not able to give a coherent response since he was drunk at the time of his arrest. (n.) coherence; (v.) cohere; (adv.) coherently
collaboration	(n.) the action of working together with others; (syn.) cooperation. e.g. - The collaboration of all the factory workers made everyone's job easier. (v.) collaborate.
colossal	(adj.) amazing or incredible in size. e.g. - The elephant is a colossal animal, often weighing several tons.
commemorate	(v.) to serve as a reminder for events of particular historical significance. e.g. - Veteran's Day is celebrated to commemorate the lives lost in former wars. (n.) commemoration; (adj.) commemorative.
commence	(v.) to begin; to start. e.g. - The T.V. program commenced at 8:00 and finished at 9:00. (n.) commencement.
commended	(adj.) deserving of special praise, acclaim, or attention. e.g. - The soldier was commended for bravery in battle by receiving a Purple Heart Medal. (n.) commendation; (v.) commend.
commentary	(n.) a systematic explanation of events. e.g. - He is a sports announcer and often provides commentary during televised football games. (n.) commentator; (v.) comment.
commercial	(adj.) relating to business or finance. e.g. - Banking and investments are commercial activities. (n.) commerce; (adv.) commercially.
commodity	(n.) any item that can be bought and sold in the marketplace. e.g. - Gold and silver are precious commodities that are readily exchanged in the marketplace.
compel	(v.) to cause or bring out through force or pressure. e.g. - His parents compelled him to attend college, although he didn't want to. (n.) compulsion; (adj.) compelling.
compendious	(adj.) relating to a publication that is comprehensive and concise. e.g. - You had better start reading that compendious book now if you want to be ready for your exams.

compensation	(n.) payment for services, loss, or injury. e.g. - He was awarded one hundred thousand dollars by the court as compensation for his injuries. (v.) compensate; (adj.) compensatory.
complacent	(adj.) describing the failure to remain diligent or aware, esp. because one has become too self-satisfied. e.g. - They got burglarized because they had become complacent and left their door unlocked. (n.) complacency; (adv.) complacently.
competent	(adj.) being capable and skilled in a particular task. e.g. - He is more than competent to repair the truck. He has done it successfully many times before. (n.) competence; (adv.) competently.
component	(n.) an integral or necessary part of sthg. e.g. - All of the components must be working in order for the machine to function properly.
compulsory	(adj.) required; necessary; obligatory; (syn.) mandatory. e.g. - Class attendance is compulsory. You are required to attend.
concatenation	(n.) the series of items linked in different orders. e.g. - There are many concatenations of human DNA. (v.) concatenate.
concoct	(v.) to make up or invent a story. e.g. - When asked why she was late for class, Marisa concocted an incredible story. (n.) concoction; (adj.) concocted.
condone	(v.) to view as unimportant; to overlook. e.g. - Your behavior is unacceptable, and I cannot condone it. (adj.) condonable.
conducive (to)	(adj.) beneficial; helpful. e.g. - A quiet weekend in the countryside is conducive to relaxation. (v.) conduce.
confine	(v.) to cause to become limited in room or space. e.g. - The prisoner was confined to his cell twenty-three hours a day and often dreamed of freedom. (n.) confinement; (adj.) confined.
confiscate	(v.) to seize or take away, especially when a person is found to have sthg illegally. e.g. - The police confiscated the drugs he was carrying when he passed through the airport. (n.) confiscation; (adj.) confiscated.
conflagration	(n.) a great fire. e.g. - The fire department was called to put out the conflagration.
conform (to)	(v.) to agree to or comply with a standard. e.g. - Those individuals who do not conform to the rules of the club will be denied membership. (n.) conformity.

consensus	(n.) agreement by members of a group. e.g. - After fifteen minutes of discussion, the group finally reached a <u>consensus</u> about what restaurant to go to. (v.) consent.
consequence	(n.) outcome or result, esp. an undesired one. e.g. - You had better consider the <u>consequences</u> of your actions if you want to be a responsible citizen. (adj.) consequential; (adv.) consequentially.
consistency	(1)(n.) texture; firmness; (2)(n.) the quality of not changing. e.g. - (1) The <u>consistency</u> of the apple was too soft. We knew that it was not fit to eat. (2) Brandy has shown <u>consistency</u> in her performance at college this year. She has received A's all semester. (adj.) consistent; (adv.) consistently.
console	(v.) to soothe or comfort. e.g. - Terri was crying, so we tried to <u>console</u> her by saying that everything was going to be alright. (n.) consolation.
consolidate	(v.) to join together; unite; merge. e.g. - The two companies <u>consolidated</u> to form a new, larger company. (n.) consolidation; (adj.) consolidated.
conspicuous	(adj.) noticeable; capable of drawing attention. e.g. - Tim's wealth was <u>conspicuous</u> by the large amounts of money he spent. (n.) conspicuousness; (adv.) conspicuously.
constituent	(n.) a citizen of a particular political district who is eligible to vote in elections. e.g. - The <u>constituents</u> of Dallas will vote for a new mayor in the upcoming elections. (n.) constituency.
contaminate	(v.) to cause to become infected, polluted, or poisoned. e.g. - Many American rivers used to be <u>contaminated</u> by pollution from nearby factories. (n.) contamination.
contemplate	(v.) to think about or consider. e.g. - The great philosophers often <u>contemplated</u> the meaning of life. (n.) contemplation; (adj.) contemplative; (adv.) contemplatively.
contempt	(n.) hatred or disgust; (syn.) enmity. e.g. - Great <u>contempt</u> was shown towards the criminal by the judge, who said that the crimes shocked society. (adj.) contemptible, contemptuous.
contend (with)	(v.) to deal with; to manage a difficult situation. e.g. - Police officers have to <u>contend</u> with danger and violence in their jobs. (n.) contention.
contiguous	(adj.) adjoining; neighboring; sharing a common boundary. e.g. - The northern border of the United States is <u>contiguous</u> with Canada. (n.) contiguity; (adv.) contiguously.

contingent	(adj.) dependent upon unpredictable causes or events. e.g. - Our trip to the beach tomorrow is <u>contingent</u> upon the weather. (n.) contingency; (adv.) contingently.
contravene	(v.) to oppose or act against the desires or wishes of another individual. e.g. - Children who <u>contravene</u> the wishes of their parents often receive punishment. (n.) contravention.
contrition	(n.) the feeling of deep sorrow or regret about one's wrong-doings; (syn.) remorse, penitence. e.g. - The criminal felt great <u>contrition</u> for his crimes and was filled with regret. (adj.) contrite.
contrive	(v.) to devise, plan, or premeditate. e.g. - After months of planning, the prisoners finally <u>contrived</u> a way to escape. (adj.) contrived.
convene	(v.) to meet as a group, esp. formally or officially. e.g. - The United Nations will <u>convene</u> in New York in the fall.
convivial	(adj.) cheerful; friendly. e.g. - He has a <u>convivial</u> personality and is very outgoing. (n.) conviviality; (adv.) convivially.
cordial	(adj.) friendly; (syn.) affable, amiable, winsome. e.g. - She is quite <u>cordial</u> and makes friends easily. (adv.) cordially.
coroner	(n.) a medical examiner who investigates unexpected or violent deaths. e.g. - The <u>coroner</u> pronounced the victims dead after the fatal accident.
corrugated	(adj.) relating to metal or cardboard that has been formed and strengthened by pressing it into ridges under force or pressure. e.g. - The shed has a <u>corrugated</u> iron roof. (v.) corrugate.
countenance	(n.) a person's facial expression. e.g. - You could tell by her <u>countenance</u> that she was feeling depressed.
counterfeit	(n.) false copies of paper money. e.g. - This money is <u>counterfeit</u>. It is not authentic and is, therefore, worthless. (v.) counterfeit; (adj.) counterfeit.
coup	(n.) a revolutionary group that seeks to overthrow an existing government, esp. with the use of violence. e.g. - The Parliament building was seized during the <u>coup</u> as the rebels attempted to take control of the government.
covert	(adj.) hidden or secretive. e.g. - The details of the <u>covert</u> military operation were known only to the president and a few of his close assistants. (n.) covertness; (adv.) covertly; (ant.) overt.
credential	(n.) proof of a person's identity or suitability to perform a job. e.g. - You should not let any contractors into your house unless you are sure of their <u>credentials</u>. (adj.) credentialed.

credible	(adj.) believable or trustworthy. e.g. - He was considered to be a <u>credible</u> witness as he was at the scene of the crime when it took place.
crevice	(n.) a narrow crack. e.g. - Barbara fell down when her heel got caught in a <u>crevice</u> in the sidewalk.
crimson	(adj.) dark red. e.g. - Blood is <u>crimson</u> in color.
culminate (in)	(v.) to bring to a conclusion. e.g. - The graduation ceremony <u>culminates</u> in the distribution of diplomas to the class. (n.) culmination.
cultivation	(n.) the process of preparing the land for planting; (met.) the act of fostering or mentoring. e.g. - <u>Cultivation</u> begins in the spring when the top soil is turned over in order to prepare the ground for seeds or plants. (v.) cultivate; (adj.) cultivated.
cumbersome	(adj.) troublesome; difficult; heavy. e.g. - Jennifer's journey was <u>cumbersome</u> since she carried two huge suitcases with her. (v.) encumber.
cumulative	(adj.) the total sum of separate parts. e.g. - The <u>cumulative</u> sum of 20 and 20 is 40. (v.) cumulate; (adv.) cumulatively.
cursory	(adj.) relating to doing sthg quickly and with little attention, without noticing the details; (syn.) perfunctory. e.g. - They are going to have to spend much more money on that construction project. They gave the site only a very <u>cursory</u> inspection before going ahead with the work, and now there are unexpected expenses.
custody	(n.) control or guardianship over a person by an individual in authority. e.g. - Anne was granted <u>custody</u> of the children in the divorce. They now live with her. (adj.) custodial.
cynical	(adj.) having a distrust in another person's motives or in human nature in general. e.g. - He is <u>cynical</u> about her offer to help him since she has let him down before. (n.) cynicism.

Exercises – C

Instructions: Complete the sentences below, using one of the words beginning with the letter "C" from the previous section. Note that some gaps may have more than one possible answer. You may also need to change the form of the word. The answers are provided at the end of book.

1) You are certainly going to be severely _____ for speaking to your commanding officer in such a disrespectful way.

2) The boat _____, and the passengers fell into the ocean.

3) All candidates should be _____ of the fact that the training program is very demanding.

4) If you only study in a _____ way, you will never pass your exam.

5) They had a _____ relationship and had to meet in secret places.

6) The _____ of the members of staff will ensure that the project is completed more quickly.

7) Your parents would never _____ you behaving in such an outrageous way.

8) After weeks of refusing my request, my boss finally _____ and said I could take my vacation when I wanted.

9) He knew that he would be reprimanded if he was caught _____ in public.

10) She couldn't put forward a _____ argument for her point of view, so we weren't convinced that her idea was a good one.

Words – D

Instructions: Study the words below, paying attention to their meanings as well as how they are used in the example sentences. Then complete the exercise that follows.

datum	(n.) a single piece of information. In engineering, the line or point used for measuring elevations. (pl.) data. e.g. - The machine provides an accurate datum that is worth taking into account in our calculations.
debonair	(adj.) sophisticated, stylish, or cultured. e.g. - He is very well-mannered. I have never met such a charming and debonair man.
debouch	(n.) a passage from which troops emerge. (v.) to emerge from such a passage. e.g. - The troops will debouch from the wooded passage at the side of the valley.
debris	(n.) the remaining broken pieces of sthg. e.g. - There was a lot of debris on the road after the accident, including fragments of broken glass and pieces of metal.
deceased	(adj.) relating to a person who has died. e.g. - My father is deceased. He died ten years ago. (n.) decedent.
deciduous	(adj.) relating to trees which lose their leaves seasonally. e.g. - Deciduous trees in Vermont turn to beautiful shades of red, orange, and yellow before losing their leaves every fall.
decorous	(adj.) correct in behavior; in good taste. e.g. - The firefighters behaved in a most decorous way during the blaze and cannot be blamed for the deaths that occurred. (n.) decorum; (adv.) decorously.
deduce	(v.) to draw a logical conclusion. e.g. - He deduced that it was going to rain because it was so cloudy. (n.) deduction.
de facto	(adj.) in fact or in effect. e.g. - He was the de facto parent since he was the child's legal guardian.
defect	(n.) a lack of proper function which prevents use of a machine. e.g. - The stereo had a defect in its sound system and would not play the CD properly. (adj.) defective; (adv.) defectively.
defile	(v.) to cause to become unclean or unchaste. e.g. - The environment is being defiled with all types of pollution and litter. (n.) defilement; (adj.) defiled.
defray	(v.) to bear all or part of the cost of sthg. e.g. - If you submit an expense report, the main office will defray your expenses.

deft	(adj.) possessing great skill or ability; (syn.) adept. e.g. - Paul is quite deft at the firing range. He is a great shot. (adv.) deftly.
defunct	(adj.) no longer existing or operating; no longer active. e.g. - Due to a lack of interest by its members, the club is now defunct.
defy	(v.) to accomplish sthg that is considered impossible or improper. e.g. - He defied his parents by getting married when he was only sixteen, although they had forbidden it. (n.) defiance; (adj.) defiant; (adv.) defiantly.
deliberation	(n.) careful consideration of a topic, including reasons for and against. e.g. - After careful deliberation of all the advantages and disadvantages, she finally decided to attend college. (v.) deliberate; (adj.) deliberate.
deluge	(n.) a sudden downpour of rain or water. e.g. - A sudden deluge of rain caused flooding in the city. (v.) deluge.
demeanor	(n.) behavior, manner, or temperament. e.g. - This job requires a person with a pleasant demeanor because you will constantly be working with the public.
demise	(n.) destruction or downfall. e.g. - Excessive gambling led to his demise. He lost all of his possessions as a result of his uncontrollable habit.
demoralize	(v.) to discourage; to weaken the spirit of. e.g. - Carmen was demoralized when she failed her driving test the fourth time.
denomination	(n.) size of a value of paper money. e.g. - The bank robbers stole $10,000 in $100 and $50 denominations. (v.) denominate.
denounce	(v.) to show to be false, wrong, or evil. e.g. - He denounced smoking, saying that it was a disgusting and dangerous habit. (n.) denouncement.
dense	(adj.) thick or heavy. e.g. - A dense snowfall caused the highway department to close all the roads. (adv.) densely.
deplore	(v.) to consider as deserving of contempt or disapproval. e.g. - The teacher deplored the students who hadn't done their homework and expressed her disapproval. (adj.) deplorable; (adv.) deplorably.
deprecate	(v.) to disapprove of or devalue sthg. e.g. - He deprecated the idea of getting a new car, although he secretly wished he could afford one. (n.) deprecation; (adj.) deprecating.
deranged	(adj.) mentally disturbed; insane; crazy. e.g. - Deranged individuals, such as psychopaths or sociopaths, are in need of psychological treatment. (v.) derange.

desolate	(adj.) filled with sorrow or despair as a result of loneliness; (syn.) forlorn. e.g. - Thomas felt desolate when he moved to Houston. Since he was new in town, he didn't have any friends and was often lonely. (n.) desolation; (adj.) desolating.
despicable	(adj.) deserving of hate; (syn.) odious. e.g. - The crimes that he committed are despicable, and he has many enemies. (adv.) despicably.
despondency	(n.) despair; depression. e.g. - In his despondency, he contemplated whether his life had meaning. (adj.) despondent; (adv.) despondently.
deterrent	(n.) the prevention or discouragement of illegal or improper behavior. e.g. - The death penalty is considered to be a deterrent to the commission of the crime of murder, although statistics show that the murder rate increases every year. (v.) deter.
detrimental	(adj.) to cause harm or to have a negative effect on sthg. e.g. - If you continue to eat so poorly it will have a detrimental effect on your health. (n.) detriment; (adv.) detrimentally.
didactic	(adj.) relating to that which is taught or to the behavior of a teacher. e.g. - He has been a teacher for many years, so he has great didactic skills. (n.) didacticism; (adv.) didactically.
digress	(v.) to vary from a planned course of action or speaking. e.g. - She digressed a little from her original plan. (n.) digression; (adj.) digressive.
dilatory	(adj.) tending to delay or procrastinate. e.g. - The lawyer engaged in dilatory practices in order to gain more time to prepare the case.
dilemma	(n.) a difficult situation or problem. e.g. - His dilemma is that he wants to get the job, but he doesn't want the responsibility.
diligent	(adj.) relating to the exercise of caution and determination. e.g. - You must be diligent when driving on interstate highways in order to avoid accidents. (n.) diligence; (adv.) diligently.
dilute	(v.) to add water to a mixture. e.g. - The orange juice concentrate should be diluted and mixed before serving.
disclose	(v.) to uncover or cause to become known. e.g. - The bank robber finally disclosed the location of the hidden money after undergoing extensive questioning. (n.) disclosure.
disconcerted	(adj.) very discouraged; disillusioned. e.g. - My cousin was disconcerted when he realized that his new job wasn't what he wanted after all. (v.) disconcert.

discontented	(adj.) unhappy; displeased. e.g. - Many students become discontented with college and decide to drop out. (n.) discontentment, discontent.
discord	(n.) disagreement or disharmony. e.g. - There is so much discord between the nations that an armed conflict may break out.
discrepancy	(n.) disagreement or inconsistency between or among various things. e.g. - There was a discrepancy between the two different versions of the story. (adj.) discrepant; (adv.) discrepantly.
disdain	(n.) disgust; (syn.) contempt. e.g. - He had absolute disdain for the people who had vandalized his car. (adj.) disdainful; (adv.) disdainfully.
disjointed	(adj.) lacking in sequence, order, or organization. e.g. - The professor's explanation was totally disjointed. As a result, none of the students understood him. (v.) disjoint.
dismal	(adj.) being of particularly bad quality; disastrous; (syn.) wretched. e.g. - The weather is so dismal today with all this sleet and rain. (adv.) dismally.
dismantle	(v.) to take a machine apart into pieces; disassemble. e.g. - She dismantled her furniture before moving into her new house since the individual pieces of wood would be easier to carry.
disparity	(n.) disagreement; (syn.) incongruity. e.g. - There seems to be some disparity between the story he told and the facts.
dispatch	(v.) to send, esp. quickly. e.g. - The letter was dispatched to you by courier on Thursday. (n.) dispatch.
dispense	(v.) to give out in shares or measured parts. e.g. - My parents always dispense advice without me asking for it.
disposition	(n.) mood or character. e.g. - His disposition was great today. I have never seen him so cheerful. (v.) dispose.
dissent	(n.) disagreement; conflict; controversy. e.g. - There is some dissent about what happened. Everyone seems to have a different version of the events. (v.) dissent.
dissolute	(adj.) lacking in moral standards; (syn.) licentious. e.g. Lying and cheating are dissolute habits. (n.) dissolution; (adv.) dissolutely.
divergence	(n.) separation; movement apart; disunion. e.g. - Their divergence in personal opinions causes many arguments. (v.) diverge; (adj.) divergent.

diversification	(n.) the action of providing variety. e.g. - This college offers great <u>diversification</u> to its students, with programs ranging from animal science to hair styling. (v.) diversify; (adj.) diversified.
diversion	(n.) a change of course in direction or activity. e.g. - There is a traffic <u>diversion</u> in the center of town because the road is being repaired. (v.) divert; (adj.) diverted.
docile	(adj.) submissive or acquiescent. e.g. - He is as <u>docile</u> as a puppy after he eats a big meal. (n.) docility.
dogmatic	(adj.) relating to stating principles or ideas as if they are inarguably true or correct. e.g. - She is extremely <u>dogmatic</u> in her viewpoints, so I wouldn't try to argue with her.
domestic	(adj.) relating to or coming from a specific country. e.g. - Many <u>domestic</u> American wines are produced in California. (n.) domesticity; (v.) domesticate; (adj.) domesticated.
domicile	(n.) a person's country of normal residence or place of living. e.g. - Please write your address on the section of the form entitled "<u>Domicile</u>."
domineering	(adj.) controlling or influencing excessively. e.g. - She is a <u>domineering</u> woman and is always telling her husband what to do. (n.) domination; (v.) dominate; domineer; (adv.) domineeringly.
dormant	(adj.) inactive due to suspension of normal function. e.g. - The plants remain dormant during the winter months, but they start to grow again in the spring. (n.) dormancy.
droll	(adj.) humor that is expressed in a matter-of-fact or self-mocking manner. e.g. - He amuses all of his friends with his <u>droll</u> sense of humor.
dubious	(adj.) doubtful in quality. e.g. - He told us a <u>dubious</u> story about a series of unbelievable events that he claimed had caused his delay. (n.) dubiety, dubiousness; (adv.) dubiously.
dulcet	(adj.) sweet-sounding. e.g. - We just love the <u>dulcet</u> tones of your singing.
duplicitous	(adj.) relating to living a deceptive or double life. e.g. - The <u>duplicitous</u> man had two wives, neither of whom knew of the other's existence. (adv.) duplicitously.
dwindle	(v.) to decrease in size or amount. e.g. - The size of the class has <u>dwindled</u>. We began with twenty-five students and now have only five. (adj.) dwindling.

| dysfunction | (n.) failure to function properly. e.g. - The <u>dysfunction</u> in their relationship caused the couple to file for divorce.
(adj.) dysfunctional. |

Exercises – D

Instructions: Complete the sentences below, using one of the words beginning with the letter "D" from the previous section. Note that some gaps may have more than one possible answer. You may also need to change the form of the word. The answers are provided at the end of book.

1) A _____ cloud hung overhead, threatening us with rain.

2) The crime of murder is a _____ act.

3) Students must be _____ when filling in the answer sheet to be sure that they put the answers in the correct space.

4) The mechanic _____ the engine of the car in order to repair it.

5) His farm is very _____. He grows crops and also raises various types of animals.

6) The speaker _____ from the subject of travel safety when he began to talk about his holiday plans.

7) The puppy was so _____ that it would curl up on anyone's lap.

8) We just adore the _____ sound of your voice.

9) He has dedicated his life to teaching and other _____ pursuits.

10) While not officially the boss, he is the _____ manager while the boss is away.

Words – E

Instructions: Study the words below, paying attention to their meanings as well as how they are used in the example sentences. Then complete the exercise that follows.

earnest	(adj.) relating to sincerity in character. e.g. - If you are earnest when speaking about your problem, you will certainly receive support and sympathy. (n.) earnestness; (adv.) earnestly.
eccentric	(adj.) unconventional or slightly strange. e.g. - She wore a cape and tights to the party, so everyone was talking about her eccentric appearance. (n.) eccentricity.
effigy	(n.) a monument or memorial shaped in the likeness of a particular individual. e.g. - An effigy of Abraham Lincoln can be found in the center of Washington D.C.
egotist	(n.) a person who is exceptionally self-centered or conceited, to the point of lacking empathy for others. e.g. - She is such a self-absorbed egotist.
elaborate	(adj.) developed; containing many details. e.g. - He told such an elaborate story that it was impossible to remember all the details. (n.) elaboration; (v.) elaborate; (adv.) elaborately.
elated	(adj.) very pleased or happy; delighted. e.g. - She was elated when her baby was born. It was the happiest day of her life. (n.) elation; (v.) elate.
eldritch	(adj.) frightening; scary. e.g. - Why do you watch those eldritch movies? You know you always feel afraid afterwards.
elicit	(v.) to bring out; evoke. e.g. - The teacher gave the students many clues in order to elicit the correct answer. (n.) elicitation. Note: Do not confuse with illicit.
elite	(adj.) relating to a limited group; (syn.) exclusive. e.g. - The Beverly Hills Hotel is used only by an elite group of people, including famous movie stars.
eloquent	(adj.) well-spoken, fluent, or persuasive. e.g. - He gave an eloquent speech at his brother's wedding. (n.) eloquence; (adv.) eloquently
elusive	(adj.) impossible to be accomplished or maintained. e.g. - Her dream of becoming a marine has proven to be elusive because she could not achieve the required scores on her exams. (n.) elusion; (n.) elusiveness; (v.) elude; (adv.) elusively.

embezzle	(v.) to use one's own position to steal company money or property for personal use. e.g. - The company's accountant had been embezzling money for years by transferring it from the company's bank to his own personal account. (n.) embezzlement; (adj.) embezzled.
emblem	(n.) logo, badge, or symbolic object. e.g. - The bald eagle is one of America's national emblems.
embonpoint	(n.) excessive fullness or plumpness. Often used to refer to a woman's bosom. e.g. - She wore a low-cut, tight-fitting dress to the cocktail party, with her embonpoint on display.
embroil	(v.) to cause to become involved in a conflict. e.g. - She became embroiled in the argument by telling a different version of events.
eminent	(adj.) showing superiority or high achievement in one's profession. e.g. - The professor was eminent in the field of micro-biology and had written several well-known books on the subject. Note: Do not confuse with "imminent."
emission	(n.) to give off or send out light, sound, or smell. e.g. - The emission of poisonous gases into the atmosphere is illegal. (v.) emit.
emulate	(v.) to imitate or equal in quality. e.g. - Your brother is a perfect child. You should try to emulate him. (n.) emulation; (adj.) emulate.
encompass	(v.) to involve or include; (syn.) encompass. e.g. - Business Studies encompass the subjects of marketing and economics.
endorse	(v.) to openly express approval or support; ratify; (syn.) back. e.g. - The budget reductions that the manager proposed were not endorsed by the company. (n.) endorsement; (adj.) endorsed.
endowment	(n.) gift or contribution of money for support of an activity. e.g. - The millionaire contributed a substantial endowment towards the building of the new hospital. (v.) endow; (adj.) endowed.
enervating	(adj.) exhausting. e.g. - Running a marathon is an enervating experience and requires several days of rest afterwards. (n.) enervate.
engulf	(v.) to be consumed or totally overcome by sthg. e.g. - The fire department could not save the building since it was already engulfed in flames when they arrived.

enmity	(n.) hatred; (syn.) contempt. e.g. - They hardly parted as friends. In fact, I'd say she feels <u>enmity</u> towards him.
ensign	(n.) a flag which indicates nationality; (syn.) banner. e.g. - The <u>ensign</u> of the United States is red, white, and blue.
entail	(v.) to involve or include. e.g. - Sarah's new job as manager <u>entails</u> many responsibilities.
enterprise	(n.) a business organization established for a particular purpose or activity. e.g. - Banks and insurance companies are business <u>enterprises</u>. (adj.) enterprising.
entice	(v.) to attract by persuasion or influence; (syn.) lure. e.g. - The advertisement in the store window <u>enticed</u> him to go inside. (n.) enticement; (adj.) enticing.
entity	(n.) a business or enterprise. e.g. - A partnership is one type of business <u>entity</u>.
entreat	(v.) to beg; (syn.) beseech; implore. e.g. - The organization <u>entreated</u> the public to give donations to charity. (n.) entreaty.
enunciate	(v.) to speak in a clear and understandable way. e.g. - You will never get a job speaking on the phone if you cannot <u>enunciate</u> your words more distinctly. (n.) enunciation; (adj.) enunciated.
ephemeral	(adj.) relating to sthg that lasts for a relatively short time. e.g. - The fleeting days of the late summer are an <u>ephemeral</u> pleasure. (n.) ephemera.
epitome	(n.) the highest or best example of sthg. e.g. - With all of the volunteering that she does, she is the <u>epitome</u> of goodness.
equivocation	(n.) the action of speaking in a way that is likely to cause confusion or misunderstanding, which is done in order not to commit to a definite decision. e.g. - The lawyer spoke with <u>equivocation</u>, saying that the product was not dangerous, nor was it safe. (v.) equivocate; (adj.) equivocal; (adv.) equivocally; (ant.) unequivocal.
err	(v.) to make a mistake. e.g. - If you <u>err</u> when filling out the form online, you will need to begin again since you can't go back to the previous screens. (n.) error; (adj.) erroneous; (adj.) erroneously.
erratic	(adj.) unpredictable; inconsistent. e.g. - Her moods are so <u>erratic</u>. You never know if she'll be happy or upset. (adv.) erratically.
eulogy	(n.) kind words said at the time of someone's death or funeral. e.g. - The minister gave a <u>eulogy</u> at the funeral ceremony.

evasive	(adj.) to avoid doing sthg, often by illegal means. e.g. - He evaded income tax by keeping his money in a secret bank account in the Bahamas. (n.) evasion; (v.) evade; (adv.) evasively.
exacerbate	(v.) to make worse or more severe. e.g. - He exacerbated the fire by throwing gasoline on it. (n.) exacerbation.
exalt	(v.) to give praise; laud and glorify. e.g. - The soldier was exalted for the bravery he displayed in battle.
exasperation	(n.) a state of extreme irritation or annoyance. e.g. - He felt exasperation when the building collapsed while he was just finishing the repairs. (v.) exasperate; (adj.) exasperated, exasperating; (adv.) exasperatingly.
exempt	(adj.) to be free from a rule or obligation that is normally imposed upon the group. e.g. - If you have already taken the exam, you will be exempt from taking it again. (n.) exemption; (adj.) exempted.
exertion	(n.) excessive physical activity. e.g. - Much exertion was required to climb the mountain. Afterwards, the climbers were exhausted. (v.) exert; (adj.) exerting.
exile	(v.) to expel or force to leave, esp. one's country of origin. e.g. - She was exiled from government office due to her political viewpoints. (n.) exile.
exonerate	(v.) to clear from accusation or responsibility. e.g. - A finding of "not guilty" exonerates a suspect from all responsibility for a crime. (n.) exoneration.
exorbitant	(adj.) excessive in quantity or price; (syn.) extortionate. e.g. - You paid $5 for a candy bar. What an exorbitant price. (n.) exorbitance; (adv.) exorbitantly.
expel	(v.) to force to leave school, usually for misbehavior. e.g. - He was expelled from high school for starting a fire in the classroom. (n.) expulsion; (adj.) expelled.
explicit	(adj.) directly stated or shown, leaving no room for doubt. e.g. - How could you do that when I gave you explicit instructions to do the opposite? (n.) explicitness; (adv.) explicitly.
exploit	(v.) to use or manipulate another person for one's own purposes. e.g. - Don't let him exploit you. He's only using you for money and a place to stay. (n.) exploitation.
extenuating	(adj.) relating to lessening the seriousness of a charge; mitigating. e.g. - The use of self-defense is an extenuating circumstance against the charge of murder. (v.) extenuate.

extermination	(n.) the action of killing insects or rodents. e.g. - After discovering several mice in our kitchen, it was necessary to call a company into our home for <u>extermination</u>. (v.) exterminate.
extortionate	(adj.) excessively expensive; (syn.) exorbitant. e.g. - He paid the <u>extortionate</u> price of $5000 for a pair of tennis shoes. (adv.) extortionately.
extract	(v.) to remove. e.g. - The information you need can be <u>extracted</u> from this book. (n.) extract, extraction; (adj.) extracted.
extraneous	(adj.) irrelevant or unrelated. e.g. - You can ignore that paragraph of the document because it is <u>extraneous</u>.

Exercises – E

Instructions: Complete the sentences below, using one of the words beginning with the letter "E" from the previous section. Note that some gaps may have more than one possible answer. You may also need to change the form of the word. The answers are provided at the end of book.

1) Success proved to be _____ to him, and he couldn't realize his dream of becoming a professional football player.

2) The last few weeks of the semester are _____. I get very little sleep because I am preparing so many assignments and essays.

3) The business _____ had corporate offices in the same building.

4) I know she is angry at you, but don't _____ the situation by telling her that she is foolish.

5) You can get an excused absence from class if there are _____ circumstances.

6) Preparing for a party _____ many small details.

7) An _____ of the man who founded the town can be found in the park.

8) He continued to watch _____ movies late at night, even though they gave him nightmares.

9) The manager was fired for _____ from the company bank account.

10) Everyone wished that she would stop _____ and just say exactly what she thought.

Words – F

Instructions: Study the words below, paying attention to their meanings as well as how they are used in the example sentences. Then complete the exercise that follows.

fabricate	(v.) manufacture; (syn.) assemble. e.g. - Al fabricated a huge story which was made of lies. (n.) fabrication; (adj.) fabricated.
façade	(n.) the face of a building; (met.) an outward appearance. e.g. - The façade of the building hid the fact that it was quite ugly inside.
facetious	(adj.) relating to inappropriate humor or jokes. e.g. - When I said that Tom Cruise was my cousin, I was only being facetious. I never thought that you would take me seriously. (adv.) facetiously.
facilitate	(v.) to assist the progress of sthg or make it less difficult. e.g. - My plans to attend college were facilitated by a rich uncle who decided to pay my tuition.(n.) facilitation; (adj.) facilitated, facilitating.
fallacious	(adj.) incorrect as a result of being based on false theories or beliefs. e.g. - The theory that the earth is flat is totally fallacious. (n.) fallacy; (adv.) fallaciously.
fallible	(adj.) capable of making a mistake. e.g. - All human beings can make mistakes. Even so-called experts are fallible.
fasting	(adj.) relating to the state of having gone without food for several hours or days. e.g. - You will need to give a fasting blood sample in the morning so that your blood-sugar level is low.
fatality	(n.) a death caused by an accident or natural disaster. e.g. - Three fatalities resulted from the road accident. A man, woman, and child were reported dead. (adj.) fatal; (adv.) fatally.
fathom	(v.) to understand or comprehend, esp. with difficulty. e.g. - I can't fathom this chemistry homework. Can you explain it to me? (adj.) fathomable; (ant.) unfathomable.
feasible	(adj.) describing sthg that can be done easily or conveniently. e.g. - It should be feasible to travel there and back in one day because they live only fifty miles from us. (n.) feasibility; (adv.) feasibly.
feat	(n.) accomplishment. e.g. - Receiving a college degree by the age of thirteen is quite an amazing feat.

fecund	(adj.) fertile or productive. e.g. - The seeds grew quickly in the <u>fecund</u> soil. (n.) fecundity.
feeble	(adj.) lacking in strength, esp. as a result of old age. e.g. - Anne's grandmother is quite <u>feeble</u> and cannot lift heavy objects. (adv.) feebly.
fervid	(adj.) showing extreme enthusiasm or passion. e.g. - He is a <u>fervid</u> fan of the local baseball team. He never misses a game. (n.) fervor.
fetter	(v.) to tie up or chain. (met.) to restrict; to prevent the progress of. e.g. - Being the mother of four young children, she is <u>fettered</u> with responsibility. (n.) fetter.
fiasco	(n.) a complete failure, esp. one that causes humiliation. e.g. - Her performance during the play was a <u>fiasco</u> because she forgot all of her lines.
fickle	(adj.) changeable or inconstant; capricious. e.g. - She is a very <u>fickle</u> girl and constantly changes her mind.
fidelity	(n.) trust, faith, or confidence in or to a person or a course of action; (syn.) steadfastness. e.g. - The police officer has the strictest <u>fidelity</u> to the course of justice.
fidget	(v.) to move around restlessly. e.g. - Young children often <u>fidget</u> if they have been sitting in one place for too long. (adj.) fidgeting.
flank	(v.) to be located on both sides of someone or sthg. e.g. - Our house is <u>flanked</u> by a grocery store on the east and a parking lot on the west.
flaunt	(v.) to show or display sthg obviously or pretentiously. e.g. - She <u>flaunted</u> her new diamond ring by waving her hand in front of my face. (adj.) flaunted.
flaw	(n.) an imperfection in appearance or function. e.g. - The jacket had a serious <u>flaw</u> since one sleeve was longer than the other. (adj.) flawed.
florescent	(adj.) capable of flowering. e.g. - She picked wild flowers in the <u>florescent</u> meadow. (n.) florescence. Note: Do not confuse with "fluorescent," which means giving off light or radiation.
flounder	(v.) to work without obtaining results; to struggle. e.g. - Chris really <u>floundered</u> during his first few weeks on the job since his boss did not provide any instructions or assistance. (adj.) floundering.

flourish	(v.) to reach the highest state of activity or development. e.g. - Flowers flourish if they are grown in the warmth of a greenhouse.
fluctuate	(v.) to change back and forth. e.g. - The weather often fluctuates between hot and cold at this time of year. (n.) fluctuation.
foil	(v.) to thwart or prevent the progress of. e.g. - The bank robber's plan was foiled when the security alarm went off. (adj.) foiled.
forage	(v.) to search for sthg, including food or provisions. e.g. - She was foraging in her disorganized closet, looking for old mementos.
foremost	(adj.) the most important or noteworthy. e.g. - First and foremost, you must always be honest.
forerunner	(n.) current authority or leader. e.g. - Coca-Cola is a forerunner in the soft drink industry.
foreshadow	(v.) to indicate future events; to portend. e.g. - The offenses he committed in his youth foreshadowed his inability to fit into society later in life.
forlorn	(adj.) loneliness and despair; (syn.) desolate. e.g. - He felt forlorn after his father died. (n.) forlornness; (adv.) forlornly.
fortitude	(n.) strength; courage. e.g. - He showed great fortitude in saving the drowning man from the raging river. (v.) fortify; (adj.) fortified.
fortuitous	(adj.) happening by chance or accident; unplanned. e.g. - I had a fortuitous meeting with an old friend today. By coincidence, we both happened to be in the doctor's office at the same time. (adv.) fortuitously.
foster	(v.) to adopt or encourage; nurture. e.g. - You'd feel more optimistic if you fostered a positive attitude.
fraternal	(adj.) acting like brothers, friends, or equals. e.g. - They belong to a fraternal organization called "The Brotherhood." (n.) fraternity; (v.) fraternize.
fraudulent	(adj.) based on trickery or dishonesty. e.g. - His offer to make you president of his company is entirely fraudulent since no such company exists. (n.) fraud; (adv.) fraudulently.
fraught	(adj.) to be full of sthg. e.g. - He is fraught with nervousness these days about his upcoming wedding.
frivolous	(adj.) without seriousness or importance. e.g. - It was frivolous of her to complain about losing such a small amount of money. (n.) frivolity.

frontier	(n.) an unclaimed or unsettled area or territory. e.g. - Outer space is an unexplored frontier.
frugal	(adj.) to be very restrictive with money or in spending. e.g. - Isabel is very frugal as she is living on a pension.
fruitful	(adj.) relating to sthg which is very productive. e.g. - I had a fruitful afternoon at the office. I finished all of my work. (adv.) fruitfully.
fugitive	(n.) an individual who has escaped or is running from the law. e.g. - Charles escaped from prison five years ago and now lives his life hiding as a fugitive.
fulsome	(adj.) abundant or excessive. e.g. - He received fulsome praise for returning the lost money. (n.) fulsomeness; (adv.) fulsomely.
fume	(1)(n.) vapor; (syn.) exhaust; (2)(met.) to be very angry. e.g. - (1) - The odor from this paint is so strong that I am getting a headache from the fumes. (2) He was fuming after I insulted him.
fundamental	(adj.) basic; (syn.) rudimentary. e.g. - The law of gravity is one of the fundamental rules of physics. (adv.) fundamentally.
furlough	(n.) leave of absence, esp. when granted by the armed services; (syn.) hiatus. e.g. - He is on a six week furlough, but then he has to return to active duty.
furor	(n.) outcry or protest about sthg. e.g. - There was a furor when the country announced that it was going to raise real estate taxes.
furtherance	(n.) the act of advancing. e.g. - Failing to report to your post on time will not help the furtherance of your career.
futile	(adj.) relating to sthg that is pointless of ineffective. e.g. - Your efforts to stop the aging process are futile. Everyone grows older. (n.) futility; (adv.) futilely.

Exercises – F

Instructions: Complete the sentences below, using one of the words beginning with the letter "F" from the previous section. Note that some gaps may have more than one possible answer. You may also need to change the form of the word. The answers are provided at the end of book.

1) She was being _____. She didn't mean what she said.

2) The private was _____ by a soldier on his right and another on his left.

3) I had a _____ encounter with my cousin at the mall today. It was such a coincidence. I didn't even know she was going shopping.

4) It is _____ to complain about such a small, insignificant problem.

5) The _____ principles of geometry state that a right angle will always have ninety degrees.

6) The orchestra paid _____ tribute to the composer by playing all of his concertos.

7) Children _____ if given love, care, discipline, and support.

8) Our plans for vacation were _____ when a hurricane hit the resort area.

9) The concert was a complete _____. It was so bad that most of the audience had already left after just three songs.

10) Everyone thinks that idea is true, but in fact it is _____ .

Words – G to H

Instructions: Study the words below, paying attention to their meanings as well as how they are used in the example sentences. Then complete the exercise that follows.

gait	(n.) an individual's style of running, walking, or stepping. e.g. - He finished the race first because he ran with the fastest gait.
galvanize	(v.) to strengthen by coating with a protective layer, esp. sthg made of metal. (met.) to shock or disturb someone. e.g. - The invasion by US troops galvanized the country into action. (n.) galvanization; (adj.) galvanized.
garbled	(adj.) confused or unclear in meaning. e.g. - He left a garbled message that no one could understand. (v.) garble.
garish	(adj.) the quality of being displayed excessively or tastelessly. e.g. - The interior decorations of their house were garish: red carpeting, orange curtains, and a purple sofa. (adv.) garishly.
garner	(v.) to gain or gather. e.g. - Abraham Lincoln garnered support during the U.S. Civil war.
garrison	(n.) a fort, fortress, or military post. (n.) the troops that occupy such a fortress. e.g. - The troops were stationed in a garrison in order to defend the nearby town.
garrulous	(adj.) talkative; outgoing; (syn.) gregarious, ebullient. e.g. - He is so garrulous that sometimes it's difficult to make him stop talking. (adv.) garrulously.
genial	(adj.) polite, well-mannered. e.g. - He is very genial. Not once have I heard him speak in a rude or impolite way. (adv.) genially.
genocide	(n.) the act of killing large groups of people, esp. those of a particular ethnic background. e.g. - Hitler is infamous for his genocide of the Jewish people during World War II.
ghastly	(adj.) terrible or shocking. e.g. - He had a ghastly look on his face after he witnessed the accident.
gimmick	(n.) a trick or feature used to attract to attention. e.g. - Free gifts or samples are often included with new products as a gimmick to entice the customer to buy them.
glum	(adj.) without hope; depressed. e.g. - Bruce is really glum these days. He is unhappy about failing his exams again. (adv.) glumly.

glut	(n.) an excess or overabundance of sthg. e.g. - Fuel prices have dropped due to the glut of petroleum in international markets.
gnaw	(v.) to chew on, esp. continuously. e.g. - The rats were gnawing on the wood with their teeth.
goad	(v.) to influence or provoke someone, esp. to take a course of action. e.g. - His friends goaded him into stealing the cigarettes.
grating	(adj.) irritable or unpleasant in sound or feeling. e.g. - She has such a grating voice that I find it hard to listen to her. (v.) grate.
grumble	(v.) to complain; (syn.) whine. e.g. - There is no reason to grumble about your job. If you don't like it, find a new one. (n.) grumble.
guileless	(adj.) innocent, sincere, or incapable of deception; (syn.) ingenuous. e.g. - It seems impossible that he could be lying. He looks so vulnerable and guileless. (ant.) disingenuous.
habitant	(n.) an inhabitant or resident. e.g. - He is a habitant of Chicago because his main residence is there.
habitat	(n.) a living space or environment. e.g. - Wet soil is the usual habitat for worms.
hale	(adj.) fit and hearty. e.g. - He is a hale and hearty man in the prime of his life.
hamlet	(n.) a small town or village. e.g. – Two hundred years ago, this town was a small hamlet, but now it's a huge city.
haughty	(adj.) overly proud or snobbish. e.g. - She was haughty about winning first prize in the contest. (adv.) haughtily.
hearth	(n.) the floor of a fireplace. e.g. - The fire was burning in the hearth.
hearty	(adj.) relating to physical strength and good health; (syn.) strapping. e.g. - Regular exercise and healthy food will make you hearty. (n.) heartiness; (adv.) heartily.
hectic	(adj.) exceptionally active or busy. e.g. - What a hectic day. I haven't had a moment to rest. (adv.) hectically.
heinous	(adj.) exceptionally shocking or horrible. e.g. - The murder of the young children was a heinous crime and should be punished severely.
helm	(n.) a wheel by which a ship or vessel is controlled. (met.) a place of command or control. e.g. - The director is at the helm of the company.

hindrance	(n.) the action of holding back, delaying, or preventing the progress of sthg; (syn.) obstacle; stumbling block. e.g. - His constant interruptions were a hindrance to the completion of the job. (v.) hinder.
hindsight	(n.) the understanding of the consequences of an event after it has occurred. e.g. - With hindsight, he realizes the mistakes he has made in his past.
hoarse	(adj.) unpleasant or rough in sound. e.g. - My brother is hoarse from shouting too much at the football game last night. (adv.) hoarsely.
hoax	(n.) a fictitious report of a sighting or event. e.g. - His report of viewing an aircraft from outer-space was a total hoax.
hoist	(v.) to lift or raise, often with equipment or machinery. e.g. - The sailors hoisted the sail into place.
hostile	(adj.) aggressive or adversarial. e.g. - We are entering hostile enemy territory tomorrow, so we expect to be fired upon. (n.) hostility.
hunch	(n.) an instinctive feeling or idea. e.g. - I didn't have any proof that he was lying. It was only a hunch.
hurl	(v.) to throw with great force or strength. e.g. - The baseball player hurled the ball to his teammate, who caught it.
hyperbole	(n.) an obvious exaggeration. e.g. - He said he waited forever for me to arrive, but that is sheer hyperbole. (adj.) hyperbolic.
hypocrisy	(n.) insincerity; pretending to have moral standards, when one does not. e.g. - He told his employees not to steal, but he embezzled a million dollars from his former company. Talk about hypocrisy!
hypocrite	(n.) a person who pretends to have moral standards, but does not. e.g. - He told his employees not to steal, but he embezzled a million dollars from his former company. He's such a hypocrite!

Exercises – G to H

Instructions: Complete the sentences below, using one of the words beginning with the letters "G" or "H" from the previous section. Note that some gaps may have more than one possible answer. You may also need to change the form of the word. The answers are provided at the end of book.

1) There is a _____ of that product nowadays because supply has totally outstripped demand.

2) The perpetrator should be sentenced to life in prison for such a _____ crime.

3) I don't think she would lie to you because she seems completely _____.

4) She _____ constantly about her boyfriend. If she is so unhappy, she should leave him.

5) He is a _____ because he tells everyone to come to work on time, but then he always sneaks in an hour late through the back door.

6) If you shout too much you will become _____.

7) The ship sailed smoothly through the sea with the experienced captain at the _____.

8) The police officer didn't have any evidence to charge the suspect with the crime. He only had a _____.

9) The instructions were _____ , so we couldn't understand what we needed to do.

10) He is a very _____ person. He is always so talkative and outgoing.

Words – I

Instructions: Study the words below, paying attention to their meanings as well as how they are used in the example sentences. Then complete the exercise that follows.

idle	(adj.) inactive or non-functioning. e.g. - The plant is closed because it is <u>idle</u> this month.
ignite	(v.) to start a fire. e.g. - The police investigation determined that the fire had been <u>ignited</u> with gasoline. (n.) ignition.
illicit	(adj.) illegal. e.g. - <u>Illicit</u> drugs, such as heroin and cocaine, have become a serious problem of modern society. (adv.) illicitly. (ant.) licit.
illusion	(n.) a false or misleading view of reality; (syn.) misapprehension. e.g. - She was under the <u>illusion</u> that she could spend all the money she wanted, although in reality she was on the verge of bankruptcy. Note: Do not confuse with "allusion."
illustrious	(adj.) outstanding, distinguished, or famous. e.g. - He is known around the world for his <u>illustrious</u> career as an astronaut. (n.) illustriousness; (adv.) illustriously.
immaculate	(adj.) exceptionally clean or tidy. e.g. - Her house was so <u>immaculate</u> that no dust or dirt could be seen. (adv.) immaculately.
immense	(adj.) huge or extensive. e.g. - You wrote a two-thousand page book. That must have required an <u>immense</u> amount of work. (adv.) immensely.
immerse	(v.) to dip or plunge entirely in water or fluid. (met.) to be deeply involved in sthg. e.g. - He is totally <u>immersed</u> in his business nowadays. He has no free time at all. (n.) immersion.
immutable	(adj.) describing sthg that cannot be changed or diminished. e.g. - The fact that the sun rises in the east is an <u>immutable</u> truth. (n.) immutability; (adv.) immutably.
impair	(v.) to harm or damage. e.g. - Listening to music at extremely loud volumes can <u>impair</u> your hearing. (n.) impairment; (adj.) impaired.
impartial	(adj.) relating to treatment with fairness and equality; unbiased. e.g. - An <u>impartial</u> teacher does not have favorite students, but treats all students equally. (n.) impartiality; (adv.) impartially.
impeachable	(adj.) casting doubt on one's character, credibility, or reputation. e.g. - His motives are dubious and his character is <u>impeachable</u>.

impeccable	(adj.) without fault or blame; perfect. e.g. - I don't believe his behavior is as impeccable as you say. Nobody's perfect, you know. (adv.) impeccably.
imperative	(adj.) essential; exceptionally urgent or important. e.g. - It is imperative that this medicine be taken exactly every eight hours. Failure to do so can result in death.
impertinent	(adj.) rude and disrespectful; (syn.) insolent. e.g. - You will be sanctioned if you are impertinent to a superior officer. (n.) impertinence; (adv.) impertinently.
impervious	(adj.) describing sthg that remains unaffected or unchanged, esp. in spite of efforts to the contrary. e.g. - We tried to give her suggestions for improvement, but she was impervious to our comments. (n.) imperviousness; (adv.) imperviously.
impetus	(n.) a force or event that suddenly causes sthg; a catalyst. e.g. - Losing his job gave him the impetus to try a new career.
implement	(n.) a tool or piece of equipment used for a specific purpose. e.g. - Several implements, such as plows, are needed to harvest crops from the fields in the fall. (n.) implementation; (v.) implement.
implicate	(v.) to show proof of the commission of or involvement in a crime; (syn.) incriminate. e.g. - His possession of the gun used in the murder implicated him in the crime. (n.) implication.
implicit	(adj.) unstated or implied. e.g. - He didn't say exactly how he felt, but his views were implicit in his tone of voice. (n.) implicitness; implication; (adv.) implicitly.
implore	(v.) to beg; (syn.) entreat, beseech. e.g. - The President implored the nation for their support during the country's economic crisis. (adj.) imploring; (adv.) imploringly.
imposing	(adj.) overwhelming in size or amount. e.g. - A New York penthouse suite can cost well over $1,000,000, which is far too imposing for most people. (v.) impose.
impregnable	(adj.) incapable of being entered or penetrated. e.g. - The castle was impregnable and could not be invaded by the enemy. (n.) impregnability; (adv.) impregnably.
impropriety	(n.) improper behavior. e.g. - I can't believe you had the impropriety to say that to your commanding officer. (ant.) propriety.
inamorata	(n.) a female lover or sweetheart. e.g. - Everyone but his wife knew that he had an inamorata.

incidental	(adj.) not relating to the main part; minor. e.g. - Your comments are only incidental and will not have an effect on our final decision. (adv.) incidentally.
incinerate	(v.) to burn or destroy by fire. e.g. - We will need to incinerate the classified documents and then rake through the ashes. (n.) incinerator; (adj.) incinerated.
inclination	(n.) the desire to do, feel, or achieve sthg; (syn.) proclivity. e.g. - He had a great inclination to sleep in class as he was up all night. (adj.) inclined.
incoherent	(adj.) impossible to understand or comprehend. e.g. - Your written response to the complaint was incoherent. None of us could understand what you were saying. (ant.) coherent. (ant.) disinclination.
incognito	(adj.) in disguise; concealing one's real identity e.g. - No one could recognize him because he travels incognito.
incongruity	(n.) incompatibility or disagreement between or among things. e.g. - There is total incongruity between the lies he told and reality. (adj.) incongruous; (ant.) congruity.
inconsequential	(adj.) having no importance, significance, or effect. e.g. - We tried to stop the developers from building so many new houses in our community, but our efforts were inconsequential.
incredulous	(adj.) in a state of disbelief or skepticism. e.g. - They kept telling her that she had really won the lottery, but she remained incredulous.
incriminate	(v.) to show proof concerning the commission of or involvement in a crime; (syn.) implicate. e.g. - The presence of the attacker's blood type at the murder scene incriminated him in the crime. (n.) incrimination; (adj.) incriminating.
inculcate	(v.) to instill or teach. e.g. - My parents inculcated me with good moral values. (n.) inculcation.
indefatigable	(adj.) incapable of experiencing fatigue or exhaustion. e.g. - My boss is indefatigable. He never gets tired and is always energetic. (adv.) indefatigably.
indelible	(adj.) incapable of being erased, removed or forgotten. e.g. - The events of that weekend have left an indelible impression on my memory.
indigent	(adj.) living in conditions of poverty. e.g. - Without a home or a job, she is indigent and is living on the streets. (n.) indigence.

indignant	(adj.) feeling anger as a result of being unfairly accused of a wrongdoing. e.g. - He became indignant when he was wrongly accused of cheating on the exam. (n.) indignity; (adv.) indignantly.
indispensable	(adj.) essential; necessary. e.g. - Fresh food and water are indispensable for human survival. (n.) indispensability; (adv.) indispensably.
industrious	(adj.) relating to very hard-working individuals. e.g. - The manager received a promotion because he was so industrious.
inertia	(n.) the force which keeps at object at rest from moving. (met.) tending to do nothing or being unwilling to change. e.g. - We will need to push the car to overcome the inertia. (adj.) inert.
infirmity	(n.) the condition of being weak as a result of illness, injury, or disease. e.g. - His broken leg has never healed properly. This infirmity causes him great pain, especially when walking. (adj.) infirm.
infringement	(n.) violation. e.g. - Cheating on examinations is an infringement of the rules of this college. (v.) infringe.
infuriate	(v.) to cause to become extremely angry or irate. e.g. - Your comment that I am stupid really infuriates me. (n.) fury; (adj.) furious.
ingenious	(adj.) exceptionally intelligent, intellectual, or inventive. e.g. - Men such as Einstein and Edison were highly ingenious.
inhabitant	(n.) resident. e.g. - He has been an inhabitant of Boston for the past fifteen years. (v.) inhabit.
inheritance	(n.) the action of receiving money or specific property upon another person's death. e.g. - James received a substantial inheritance when his parents died, and he is now quite rich. (v.) inherit.
inimical	(adj.) harmful or adverse; hostile. e.g. - The United Nations attempts to improve inimical relationships among various countries through goodwill and diplomacy. (adv.) inimically.
inimitable	(adj.) unique or impossible to copy or imitate. e.g. - His unique style is inimitable. (n.) inimitability; (adv.) inimitably.
innate	(adj.) inborn; inherent. e.g. - She has innate musical talent and learned how to play the piano in only two days. (adv.) innately.

innocuous	(adj.) not causing harm or injury. e.g. - That snake is not poisonous. In fact, it is totally <u>innocuous</u>. (ant.) pernicious; insidious.
innovative	(adj.) new; novel. e.g. - This <u>innovative</u> machine is bound to replace every similar older machine currently on the market. (n.) innovation; (v.) innovate.
inquisition	(n.) the process of subjecting to questioning, esp. extensively; (syn.) interrogation. e.g. - Your mother subjected me to an <u>inquisition</u>. I have never been asked so many questions in my life. (adj.) inquisitive; (adv.) inquisitively.
insidious	(adj.) appearing in a harmless way, but causing negative effect; deceitful. e.g. - Her attempt to get to know you is an <u>insidious</u> effort to gain information that she can use to gossip about you.
insinuation	(n.) sthg that is implied, inferred, or expressed indirectly. e.g. - His <u>insinuation</u> in saying that I never attended college was that I was stupid. (v.) insinuate.
insolent	(adj.) exhibiting a lack of respect; insubordinate; impudent. e.g. - The <u>insolent</u> student told the teacher that he was stupid. (n.) insolence.
instigate	(v.) to cause or incite improper or destructive behavior. e.g. - The leader of the gang <u>instigated</u> his followers into starting the riot. (n.) instigation.
insuperable	(adj.) incapable of being surpassed or overcome; (syn.) insurmountable. e.g. - The problem with this computer system is <u>insuperable</u>. We have no choice but to abandon it and start over from the beginning. (adv.) insuperably.
insurmountable	(adj.) incapable of being overcome; (syn.) insuperable. e.g. - His problems seemed <u>insurmountable</u> and in desperation, he felt that he could not go on. (adv.) insurmountably.
interject	(v.) to interrupt, insert, or come between sthg. e.g. - Before we proceed to the next topic, I would like to <u>interject</u> with my viewpoint. (n.) interjection.
interrogation	(n.) questioning; (syn.) inquisition. e.g. - A full <u>interrogation</u> was conducted to determine the whereabouts of the stolen diamond. (v.) interrogate.
intertwine (with)	(v.) to weave. (met.) to become mutually involved in. e.g. - He became <u>intertwined</u> with crime when he agreed to participate in the robbery.

intrepid	(adj.) brave; courageous; unafraid. e.g. - The <u>intrepid</u> explorers entered the cave in darkness. (n.) intrepidity, intrepidness; (adv.) intrepidly.
intricate	(adj.) very detailed or complicated. e.g. - Advanced mathematics involves many <u>intricate</u> theories and calculations. (adv.) intricately.
intrigue	(n.) a strategic plan or scheme; (v.) to arouse the curiosity. e.g. - The political <u>intrigue</u> involved a plan to spy on enemy governments. (v.) intrigue; (adj.) intriguing; (adv.) intriguingly.
inundate	(v.) to overwhelm or overpower. e.g. - The area was <u>inundated</u> with rain in the thunderstorm last night. (n.) inundation.
invigorate	(v.) to provide energy; to stimulate. e.g. - Jogging in the fresh air always <u>invigorates</u> me. (n.) invigoration; (adj.) invigorating; (adj.) invigorated.
iota	(n.) an extremely small or miniscule amount. e.g. - You will not get the promotion. Whatever you say or do will not make an <u>iota</u> of difference.
irrevocable	(adj.) impossible to be changed, altered, or taken away. e.g. - Once you sign this agreement, it is <u>irrevocable</u> and cannot be changed in any way. (adv.) irrevocably; (ant.) revocable.

Exercises – I

Instructions: Complete the sentences below, using one of the words beginning with the letter "I" from the previous section. Note that some gaps may have more than one possible answer. You may also need to change the form of the word. The answers are provided at the end of book.

1) Her car is always _____. There is never any spot or stain on it.

2) She was _____ in the robbery because she had some of the stolen money in her bag.

3) The _____ child was incredibly rude and disrespectful to the school principal.

4) She has been an _____ of the State of Arizona for ten years.

5) Her English is _____. Her vocabulary is precise, and her grammar is always correct.

6) The political leader _____ a rebellion against the government.

7) He is always _____. He is lazy and never gets anything done.

8) The teacher _____ the students to pay attention in class.

9) Magellan was an _____ explorer. He travelled to many parts of the world without having a rest or taking a break.

10) Newton's law of gravity is an _____ truth of nature.

Words J to L

Instructions: Study the words below, paying attention to their meanings as well as how they are used in the example sentences. Then complete the exercise that follows.

jargon	(n.) technical language. e.g. - The computer instruction manual was filled with so much jargon. No one could understand it.
jaunt	(n.) a short trip for pleasure. e.g. - We went off on a jaunt to Las Vegas before starting our basic training.
jeopardy	(n.) risk or danger. e.g. - Your health will be in jeopardy if you continue smoking so much. (v.) jeopardize.
jetty	(n.) a small landing or pier where boats can be docked. e.g. - She jumped ashore and tied the boat to the jetty.
jovial	(adj.) cheerful, joyous, or jubilant. e.g. - There was a jovial atmosphere at the party. (n.) joviality; (adv.) jovially.
judicious	(adj.) careful, well-considered, and sensible; prudent. e.g. - Waiting for the storm to pass before we started to drive was a judicious decision.
jurisdiction	(n.) the authority to administer and apply laws and regulations. e.g. - The local sheriff has jurisdiction over this town.
juvenile	(n.) a person who is less than eighteen years of age. (adj.) relating to young people or immature behavior. e.g. - I find his moods and tantrums to be very juvenile.
kvetch	(v.) to complain, esp. extremely. e.g. - You will make the task more difficult if you continue to kvetch. Why don't you just keep quiet and do the work? (n.) kvetcher.
labyrinth	(n.) a maze (met.) sthg. from which there seems no clear way forward. e.g. - Trying to solve this problem is going to be difficult because of the is a labyrinth of laws and regulations.
laconic	(adj.) expressing few words; (syn.) concise. e.g. - His laconic reply was only two sentences long.
larceny	(n.) theft. e.g. - As a youngster, he stole cigarettes and committed other types of petty larceny. (n.) larcenist; (adj.) larcenous.
lag	(v.) to become delayed or fall behind. e.g. - The race was close at the beginning, but the first runner won when the second runner lagged behind.

land	(v.) to find or locate. e.g. - You should be able to <u>land</u> a job. There are hundreds of employment opportunities listed on various websites.
lassitude	(n.) tiredness; exhaustion. e.g. - The marathon runner showed great <u>lassitude</u> after finishing the race and rested on the grass nearby.
latent	(adj.) hidden; not obvious or visible. e.g. - The refrigerator had a <u>latent</u> defect that could not be discovered, even through careful examination. (adv.) latently; (ant.) patent.
laud	(n.) praise; honor. e.g. He graduated at the top of his class and received <u>laud</u> on graduation day. (v.) laud; (adj.) laudable; (adv.) laudably.
layperson	(n.) an individual possessing common knowledge on a certain subject; non-professional; non-expert. e.g. - He is a <u>layperson</u> on the subject of computers. He has no education or qualifications in that area.
legitimate	(adj.) lawful. e.g. - Those are legal funds because he earned them through a <u>legitimate</u> business. (n.) legitimacy; (adv.) legitimately.
lenient	(adj.) easy-going about or accepting of the improper behavior of another person. e.g. - Mary's mother is so <u>lenient</u>. She lets her do whatever she wants. (n.) lenience.
lethargic	(adj.) tired and sluggish. e.g. - She felt <u>lethargic</u> after running the marathon. (n.) lethargy.
liability	(n.) responsibility or obligation according to the law. e.g. - Debts which are owed to others are considered <u>liabilities</u>. (adj.) liable.
liaison	(n.) connection or communication between units of the armed forces to ensure united action. e.g. - We will form a <u>liaison</u> with another troop in order to carry out the mission. (v.) liaise.
licentious	(adj.) offensive in content or lacking in morality; (syn.) vulgar; lewd. e.g. - Movies with <u>licentious</u> subjects may only be seen by adults.
licit	(adj.) legal; lawful. e.g. - We thought he was carrying illegal narcotics, but it turns out that his prescriptions were completely <u>licit</u>. (ant.) illicit.
livid	(adj.) angry or furious. e.g. - He was <u>livid</u> when I told him he was stupid and lazy. (n.) lividity.

loathe	(v.) to hate, despise, or detest. e.g. - I <u>loathe</u> waking up early in the morning. I really can't stand it. (n.) loathing; (adj.) loath, loathsome.
lofty	(adj.) high or elevated in ideals or qualities. e.g. - He has very <u>lofty</u> ideas. Perhaps he should come down to earth a little bit.
loiter	(v.) to remain in a place without any obvious purpose. e.g. - The youngsters were just <u>loitering</u> at the convenience store. They had no real interest in buying anything.
loquacious	(adj.) eloquent or excessive in speech. e.g. - The <u>loquacious</u> principal gave a two-hour speech at the graduation ceremony. (n.) loquacity; (adv.) loquaciously.
lore	(n.) traditional beliefs held by a particular group. e.g. - The <u>lore</u> of some ancient cultures may seem difficult for us to believe nowadays.
lucrative	(adj.) relating to the production of great wealth or profit. e.g. - He was able to retire early as a result of the large sum of money he had made from <u>lucrative</u> investments. (adv.) lucratively.
ludic	(adj.) spontaneous or playful. e.g. - The author was not serious, but wrote the excerpt to cast the situation in a <u>ludic</u> light.
luminous	(adj.) giving of light; shining; (syn.) radiant. e.g. - The face of his cell phone gives off a <u>luminous</u> glow.
lure	(v.) to attract or entice. e.g. - He was <u>lured</u> into buying the car by its low price. (n.) lure.
lurk	(v.) to wait secretly in a place for the purpose of doing harm. e.g. - The criminal was <u>lurking</u> in the shadows, waiting to rob the elderly man.
lustrous	(adj.) shiny, glossy, or radiant. e.g. - She looked so healthy with her <u>lustrous</u> hair and shining eyes. (n.) luster.
luxurious	(adj.) expensive or elegant; lavish; (syn.) opulent. e.g. - We stayed in a <u>luxurious</u> hotel room, where the bathroom was done up in marble and gold. (n.) luxury.

Exercises – J to L

Instructions: Complete the sentences below, using one of the words beginning with the letters "J" to "L" from the previous section. Note that some gaps may have more than one possible answer. You may also need to change the form of the word. The answers are provided at the end of book.

1) The soldiers felt great _____ after completing the twenty mile march.

2) The cause of certain health conditions is sometimes _____ and cannot be discovered through examinations or tests.

3) The _____ speaker gave a presentation that lasted for ninety minutes.

4) Even as an adult, she is a _____ person, so she loves playing with the children.

5) All he ever does is complain. Everyone is tired of hearing him _____ .

6) He gave a _____ thank you that consisted of only seven words.

7) The report was so full of technical _____ that it was impossible to understand.

8) Businesses have many _____ and other debts to be paid.

9) That magazine is _____. It may only be seen by adults.

10) The judge has _____ over the proceedings in the case.

Words – M to O

Instructions: Study the words below, paying attention to their meanings as well as how they are used in the example sentences. Then complete the exercise that follows.

magnanimity	(n.) generosity. e.g. - The wealthy family showed great magnanimity in donating such a large sum of money to charity. (adj.) magnanimous; (adv.) magnanimously.
magnitude	(n.) degree or extent of sthg, esp. sthg large or extensive. e.g. - You had better understand the magnitude of your actions because what you decide to do will affect others.
maladroit	(adj.) completely unskilled or clumsy. e.g. - Don't ask her to dance. She is completely maladroit.
malady	(n.) disease or ailment. e.g. - Scurvy was a common malady hundreds of years ago because people did not consume enough vitamin C.
malcontent	(adj.) unhappy or dissatisfied. e.g. - The workers had not been given a break for several days and were becoming malcontent.
malice	(n.) the desire to inflict harm, esp. when caused by feelings of hatred. e.g. - The victims feel great malice towards their attacker and hope that he receives the death penalty. (adj.) malicious; (adv.) maliciously.
malign	(v.) to speak untruths about someone; to slander or defame. e.g. - If you malign someone, you could be sued for slander or libel. (adj.) maligned
mandatory	(adj.) required; necessary; obligatory; (syn.) compulsory. e.g. - Completion of this form is mandatory. It must be filled in by every applicant.
manifest	(v.) to show or display obviously. e.g. - The disease manifests itself as fever and weakness. (n.) manifestation; (adv.) manifestly.
manifold	(adj.) consisting of a wide variety; many. e.g. - She had manifold reasons for resigning from work, including personal, professional, and health-related problems.
marginal	(adj.) very small or minimal in amount; nearly unacceptable in performance. e.g. - The company will have to close down if its profits continue to be only marginal. (n.) margin; (adv.) marginally.

materialize	(v.) to appear or come into existence or reality. e.g. - Her dream of becoming a pilot failed to materialize when she was paralyzed in the accident. (n.) materialization.
maul	(v.) to brutally attack, esp. by scratching or clawing. e.g. - She was mauled by a bear when hiking in Yellowstone.
mawkish	(adj.) tearfully or foolishly emotional; (syn.) maudlin. e.g. - He started to get mawkish when we asked about his dead dog.
meager	(adj.) deficient or small in quantity. e.g. - The troops won't be able to survive more than a couple of days on these meager rations.
meander	(v.) to roam or wander. e.g. - She had lost her way and began to meander aimlessly. (adj.) meandering.
menace	(n.) threat or danger. e.g. - Drugs are a menace to the well-being of today's youth. (v.) menace; (adj.) menacing; (adv.) menacingly.
menagerie	(n.) a collection of wild or unusual animals. e.g. - Dr. Dolittle was known for having an extensive menagerie of exotic animals.
mettle	(n.) strength of character; courage. e.g. - The paramedic displayed great mettle in rescuing the man from the burning car.
militia	(n.) a group of individuals organized for the purpose of military service. e.g. - The militia carried out many exercises in order to prepare for war.
miscreant	(n.) a person who behaves badly or breaks the law. e.g. - He will never become sheriff because he is a total miscreant.
misconstrue	(v.) to misunderstand. e.g. - You have completely misconstrued what I said. When I said you looked nice today, I didn't mean that you usually don't.
misdemeanor	(n.) a criminal offense that is not serious enough to be classified as a felony. e.g. - Possessing small amounts of some drugs is classified as a misdemeanor in certain states.
mitigate	(v.) to lessen the severity of; (syn.) extenuate. e.g. - Your apology does not mitigate the seriousness of your mistake. (n.) mitigation; (adj.) mitigating; (adj.) mitigated (ant.) unmitigated.
momentous	(adj.) notable; significant; important. e.g. - His wedding day was one of the most momentous events of his life.
monetary	(adj.) relating to money, finance, or the economy. e.g. - The study of economics involves many monetary theories.

mortify	(v.) to embarrass or humiliate. e.g. - I was <u>mortified</u> because I fell down when walking across the stage to get my diploma on graduation day. (n.) mortification; (adj.) mortified.
mulct	(v.) to obtain money or possessions by fraud; to dupe. e.g. - Elderly and vulnerable people may have little awareness of swindlers, so it is possible to <u>mulct</u> them into fraudulent investments.
mundane	(adj.) relating to sthg ordinary and every-day that lacks excitement or interest. e.g. - He was bored with the <u>mundane</u> routine of his day-to-day life. (n.) mundanity; (adv.) mundanely.
municipal	(adj.) relating to the city. e.g. - The <u>municipal</u> authorities pay for the upkeep of city property. (n.) municipality.
nebulous	(adj.) unclear or ill-defined, as if cloudy. e.g. - His statements were so <u>nebulous</u> that no one could understand what he was saying. (n.) nebulosity; (adv.) nebulously.
nefarious	(adj.) extremely wicked or evil; (syn.) reprobate. e.g. - The mobsters in Chicago in the early twentieth century were <u>nefarious</u> characters.
nominate	(v.) to select a candidate for a particular duty, esp. for public office. e.g. - The class <u>nominated</u> her as their class president in the school election. (n.) nomination.
notorious	(adj.) relating to fame for despicable or blameworthy events or crimes. e.g. - He is <u>notorious</u> for having committed bank robbery, so everyone recognizes him. (n.) notoriety; (adv.) notoriously.
novice	(n.) a beginner; (syn.) neophyte. e.g. - She isn't really ready to swim in the ocean. She only learned to swim last month, so she is still a <u>novice</u>.
noxious	(adj.) the quality of possessing a poisonous or deadly gas. e.g. - Gasoline is a <u>noxious</u> substance. Breathing excessive quantities of it can cause death. (n.) noxiousness; (adv.) noxiously.
null	(adj.) without value; amounting to nothing. e.g. - A voided check is <u>null</u>. You cannot cash it.
obliterate	(v.) to wipe out or destroy; to eradicate. e.g. - Many people fear that the world may be <u>obliterated</u> by global warming. (n.) obliteration.
obscure	(adj.) difficult to understand or perceive; not plain or obvious. e.g. - He studies some <u>obscure</u> subject relating to 17th century French literature. (n.) obscurity

obsequious	(adj.) behaving like a servant; servile; obedient. e.g. - The waitress was obsequious towards the demanding customer and brought him whatever he asked for. (adv.) obsequiously.
obsolete	(adj.) relating to things which are no longer useful as a result of being replaced or becoming outdated. e.g. - Computers become obsolete quickly nowadays as they are constantly being replaced by newer models. (n.) obsolescence.
obstacle	(n.) sthg which holds back, delays, or prevents progress; impediment; (syn.) hindrance, stumbling block, barrier. e.g. - Despite the obstacle of being deaf, Beethoven was able to compose his final symphonies.
obstinacy	(n.) the action of being rigid in opinion; stubbornness. e.g. - He has displayed great obstinacy on this subject. I don't think that he's going to change his mind. (adj.) obstinate; (adv.) obstinately.
odious	(adj.) deserving of hate; (syn.) despicable. e.g. - He was convicted of the odious crime of murdering small children.
offish	(adj.) unapproachable or aloof. e.g. - The offish boy appears to be unfriendly and, as a consequence, he had few friends.
opaque	(adj.) not transparent. e.g. - That glass is opaque, so you can't see through it.
opulent	(adj.) luxurious; abundant in the display of wealth. e.g. - The king lived in an opulent palace. (n.) opulence.
ostensibly	(adv.) in appearance. e.g. - Ostensibly John is a nice guy, but when you get to know him, you realize that he isn't. (adj.) ostensible.
ostentatious	(adj.) relating to an obvious display, esp. of wealth. e.g. - It was very ostentatious of her to wear such expensive jewelry to a charity event. (adv.) ostentatiously.
overabundance	(n.) a huge or plentiful amount; more than what it necessary; (syn.) plethora. e.g. - An overabundance of rain can result in flooding.
overtone	(n.) suggestion or implication; hidden meaning. e.g. - I don't like what you are implying. The overtone is that I'm stupid.

Exercises – M to O

Instructions: Complete the sentences below, using one of the words beginning with the letters "M" to "O" from the previous section. Note that some gaps may have more than one possible answer. You may also need to change the form of the word. The answers are provided at the end of book.

1) The houses in that town were _____ by the tornado.

2) The political party _____ their candidate in the election.

3) She is so _____. I have never met anyone so stubborn.

4) He got fat due to eating a(n) _____ of food.

5) He got _____ by a bear while hunting for elk in the Tetons.

6) The large amount of donations given to charity during times of natural disaster shows the _____ of the general public.

7) Those chemicals are _____. You can die if you consume even small quantities of them.

8) Taking the foundation course is _____. Every student has to take it.

9) His tastes are very _____, and he likes to show off his wealth.

10) The court ruled that the mother's grief and rage about the murder of her daughter _____ her potential punishment for her attack on the killer.

Words – P

Instructions: Study the words below, paying attention to their meanings as well as how they are used in the example sentences. Then complete the exercise that follows.

pandemic	(n.) a widespread epidemic or incidence of disease. e.g. - There was a pandemic of bird flu in Asia a few years ago.
paradigm	(n.) an example, model, or pattern for sthg. e.g. - The business's paradigm is to acquire other failing businesses and then sell them off.
paradox	(n.) a statement that leads to a senseless or contradictory conclusion. e.g. - It is a paradox that she has discovered that she earns more money when she takes more time away from her business. (adj.) paradoxical; (adv.) paradoxically.
paramount	(adj.) highly important or significant. e.g. - If you want to get good grades, studying is paramount.
pardon	(v.) to forgive or excuse; (n.) an official release from a sentence for a crime. e.g. - The prisoner was officially pardoned by the governor and was released from jail.
parity	(n.) equality or equivalence. e.g. - There is no parity between the income of factory workers and that of company CEO's.
parsimony	(n.) the act of exhibiting excessive or extreme care about money and spending. e.g. - One example of his parsimony is that he uses his tea bags twice in order to save money. (adv.) parsimoniously; (adj.) parsimonious.
patent	(adj.) obvious; not hidden; visible. e.g. - The television had a patent defect. The crack in the screen was clearly visible. (adv.) patently; (ant.) latent.
patronize	(v.) to act as a regular customer; to provide economic support. e.g. - He regularly patronizes the restaurant on the corner. He eats there five times a week.
penchant	(n.) desire or preference; (syn.) proclivity; predilection. e.g. - He is reckless and has a penchant for participating in dangerous activities.
pending	(adj.) awaiting an official decision. e.g. - The application hasn't been processed yet, so the outcome is still pending.
pensive	(adj.) thoughtful or contemplative. e.g. - He is a very pensive person, so you can be sure that he will have thought his response out well. (adv.) pensively.

perceptible	(adj.) capable of being understood by the senses. e.g. - There has been a very perceptible change in her behavior. She used to be quite shy, but now is outspoken. (n.) perception; (v.) perceive; (adv.) perceptibly.
perfidy	(n.) disloyalty or treason toward an individual's country of national origin. e.g. - The American, Benedict Arnold, was guilty of perfidy when he told U.S. military secrets to the British during the American Revolutionary War.
perish	(v.) to die; to rot or decay. e.g. - If you don't put that fruit in the refrigerator it will perish in a few days. (adj.) perishable.
perjury	(n.) the action of lying while giving a sworn statement in court. e.g. - The witness committed perjury by saying that the suspect was with her at the time of the crime, although he was not. (v.) perjure.
permeate	(v.) to affect every aspect of sthg; to penetrate or pervade. e.g. - The smell of coffee permeated the house.
pernicious	(adj.) causing injury, hurt, or harm. e.g. - He made some pernicious comments about my business acumen that gave me self-doubts. (ant.) innocuous.
perpetual	(adj.) continuous. e.g. - I have never seen anyone as talkative as her. The conversation is perpetual. (n.) perpetuation; (v.) perpetuate; (adv.) perpetually.
perturb	(v.) to cause disorder or annoyance. e.g. - The little girl's tantrum greatly perturbed her mother. (n.) perturbation.
peruse	(v.) to read sthg, esp. carefully or for specific information. e.g. - He perused the book before deciding it was interesting enough to buy. (n.) perusal.
pervasive	(adj.) affecting all parts of sthg. e.g.- The changes to the system are pervasive; therefore, the system will need to be completely redone. (n.) pervasion, pervasiveness; (v.) pervade; (adv.) pervasively.
phlegmatic	(adj.) calm and unemotional. e.g. - He is so phlegmatic. I've never seen him get nervous under pressure. (adv.) phlegmatically.
pillage	(n.) the action of robbing or seizing objects, such as in a war. e.g. - The pillage of many stores occurred during the Los Angeles riots when much valuable merchandise was stolen. (v.) pillage.
pique	(v.) to irritate or provoke. e.g. - You piqued my curiosity by telling me that you have a surprise for me. Please tell me more.

pithy	(adj.) brief and witty. e.g. - His pithy comments made everyone laugh. (n.) pith.
pittance	(n.) a very small wage or amount of money. e.g. - He makes such a pittance at work that he can hardly feed his children.
poignant	(adj.) causing a sense of sadness or regret. e.g. - Her father's death was made more poignant by the fact that they hadn't spoken to each other in years. (adv.) poignantly.
posterity	(n.) future generations; descendants. e.g. - The rich man's fortune was quickly wasted by his posterity.
precarious	(adj.) dangerous; (syn.) treacherous. e.g. - His car was hanging off the side of the mountain in a precarious position after the accident. (n.) precariousness; (adv.) precariously.
precedent	(n.) a previous event, esp. one which establishes a pattern for subsequent behavior; (syn.) exemplar. e.g. - The judge sentenced the criminal to the death penalty. This set a precedent for the use of the death penalty for subsequent crimes. (v.) precede.
precinct	(n.) territory of a city established for police control. e.g. - New York City has many police precincts, which are usually established according to neighborhood boundaries.
precipitate	(v.) to cause or bring about, especially suddenly. e.g. - The violence precipitated full-scale war. (n.) precipitation; (adj.) precipitous.
precocious	(adj.) displaying certain talents at an early age. e.g. - Their precocious eight year old is already enrolled in college. (n.) precociousness; (adv.) precociously.
predator	(n.) an individual or animal that preys or kills. e.g. - The American black bear is a predator because it kills other animals and sometimes humans.
predicament	(n.) dilemma; difficult situation. e.g. - He was left in a predicament when his car broke down on the freeway at 4:00 a.m.
predilection	(n.) a desire or preference; (syn.) proclivity; penchant. e.g. - She has an overwhelming predilection for chocolate and always wants to eat it.
predominant	(adj.) playing a major or significant role; (syn.) prominent. e.g. - He was a predominant contributor to the hospital building fund, donating over $1,000,000. (n.) predomination; (v.) predominate; (adv.) predominantly.

preemptive	(adj.) relating to carrying out an action before others have the opportunity to do so. e.g. - The commander decided to go ahead with a preemptive strike, before the enemy was even aware of their presence. (n.) preempt; (adv.) preemptively.
prematurely	(adv.) too early. e.g. - The baby was born prematurely in March. It shouldn't have been born until May. (adj.) premature.
premise	(n.) an area of land which contains buildings. e.g. - He is a security guard at the factory. His job is to protect the premises against theft.
prerogative	(n.) a special option, decision, or privilege. e.g. - She wasn't required to attend the lesson. On the contrary, it was her prerogative.
prevalent	(adj.) commonly practiced; continuing in use or acceptance; (syn.) widespread. e.g. - Skiing is prevalent in mountainous areas. (v.) prevail; (adj.) prevalently.
procure	(v.) obtain. e.g. - The office clerk needs to procure more supplies for us. (n.) procurement; (adj.) procurable.
profane	(adj.) disrespectful of religious practices ; irreverent or obscene. e.g. - Anyone making profane comments will be removed from the courtroom. (n.) profanity.
proficient	(adj.) highly skilled or competent in a given subject or area of knowledge. e.g. - He was hired for that job in France because he is a proficient speaker of the French language. (n.) proficiency; (adv.) proficiently.
prolific	(adj.) relating to an amount which is excessive in growth or quantity; plethora. e.g. - Updike was a prolific writer. He wrote many novels in his lifetime. (n.) proliferation; (v.) proliferate; (adv.) prolifically.
prominent	(adj.) playing a major or significant role. e.g. - Your grades in high school play a prominent role in determining which college you can attend. (n.) prominence; (adv.) prominently.
prone (to)	(adj.) having a certain tendency or vulnerability. e.g. - He is clumsy and is therefore prone to accidents. (n.) proneness.
propensity	(n.) a desire or preference that appears natural to a certain person; (syn.) proclivity; predilection. e.g. - His propensity to overeat is obvious because he is so overweight. (v.) propend.
propitiate	(v.) to regain the favor of someone; to appease or placate. e.g. - After having appeared sullen in court last week, the defendant decided to testify in order to propitiate the judge and jury. (n.) propitiation; (adj.) propitiatory.

proposition	(n.) a problem put forward for consideration. e.g. - The city considered the mayor's proposition to build a new road through the city center. (v.) propose.
prosecute	(v.) to take to court for the commission of a crime. e.g. - The suspect was prosecuted in court for murder and was found not guilty. (n.) prosecution.
prosperous	(adj.) wealthy and successful. e.g. - He is a prosperous businessperson who owns three homes and several cars. (n.) prosperity
prostrate	(adj.) lying in a face-down position; sometimes used to describe an act of worship. e.g. - The patient was lying prostrate after his heart attack and had to be turned face-up so that first aid could be administered.
protocol	(n.) standards of conduct. e.g. - Protocol dictates that a sentry should always be vigilant.
protract	(v.) to continue for an extended time. e.g. - The journey was protracted by several delays as a result of the bad weather conditions.
provident	(adj.) the provision for unforeseen events in the future; careful; prudent. e.g. - It was very provident of you to bring an umbrella as rain is forecast. (n.) providence.
proviso	(n.) a condition or stipulation. e.g. - I will loan you my laptop with the proviso that you return it to me next week.
provoke	(v.) to cause or incite anger. e.g. - Her outrageous behavior provoked her father and caused him to scream and yell at her. (n.) provocation; (adj.) provocative; (adv.) provocatively.
prudence	(n.) the exercise of care or caution. e.g. - You must exercise prudence in your investments. Otherwise, you might lose a substantial amount of money. (adj.) prudent; (adv.) prudently; (ant.) imprudent.
pugnacious	(adj.) exceptionally aggressive or quarrelsome in behavior. e.g. - Sean is so pugnacious. He is always trying to start arguments. (adv.) pugnaciously.
purge	(v.) to get rid of; to cause to become empty or void. e.g. - They purged the illegal documents from their computer when they realized the authorities were observing them.
putrid	(adj.) being highly unpleasant or repugnant; rotten. e.g. - This food is putrid and is not fit to eat. (adv.) putridly.

Exercises – P

Instructions: Complete the sentences below, using one of the words beginning with the letter "P" from the previous section. Note that some gaps may have more than one possible answer. You may also need to change the form of the word. The answers are provided at the end of book.

1) She was very _____ when she spoke to the group. She didn't appear nervous at all.

2) Small villages were often _____ in the Middle Ages as attackers and raiders stole the possessions of the local people.

3) The _____ woman never gave anyone a present because she wanted to save her money.

4) You look _____ today. What are you thinking so deeply about?

5) The child was lying in a _____ position after the accident.

6) The commander said that there would be a _____ strike on the enemy before they could attack us first.

7) He is guilty of _____ because he is a secret double agent for both countries.

8) The completion of the project was _____ by several months because of a lack of financing.

9) There has been a _____ shift in the attitude of the class after the teacher told us off. Some students used to disrespect the teacher, but they don't anymore.

10) He found that the holiday season was always a _____ reminder of his father's absence.

Words – Q to R

Instructions: Study the words below, paying attention to their meanings as well as how they are used in the example sentences. Then complete the exercise that follows.

quaint	(adj.) charming and old-fashioned. e.g. - The old-fashioned Austrian village had a quaint atmosphere.
qualm	(n.) doubt, worry, or uncertainty. e.g. - We let our son travel overseas on his own, although we had several qualms about it.
quandary	(n.) a state of uncertainty or confusion about what to do in a difficult situation. (syn.) dilemma. e.g. - He was in a quandary because he did not get accepted into any of the colleges to which he had applied.
querulous	(adj.) characterized by constant complaining. e.g. - The man became querulous in old age and began to complain about everything. (n.) querulousness; (adv.) querulously.
query	(n.) a question or inquiry. (v.) to ask or inquire about sthg. e.g. - We had a query from the editor of the magazine, asking us whether we would change the title of our article.
quiescence	(n.) the action of being still, motionless, or at rest. e.g. - There were periods of revolt in the warring country, which were usually followed by weeks of quiescence. (adj.) quiescent.
radical	(adj.) extreme; non-conservative; non-traditional. e.g. - He has radical political theories. In fact, he believes that the government should be abolished entirely. (adv.) radically.
raffish	(adj.) disreputable or vulgar; (syn.) dissolute. e.g. - Tabloid magazines shows that some movie stars have very raffish behavior.
rancid	(adj.) having a bad smell or taste. e.g. - You had better not eat that food. It is rancid. (n.) rancidity, rancidness.
ransack	(v.) to throw into disorder or disorganization as a result of searching for valuables, esp. during a burglary. e.g. - The burglars ransacked the house in search of jewelry and money. (adj.) ransacked.
rapport	(n.) a harmonious and sympathetic relationship which has good communication. e.g. - There is a good rapport between the two nations, so it seems likely that there will be no problems in signing the treaty.

ravage	(v.) to cause severe and extensive damage. e.g. - The hurricane <u>ravaged</u> the southern coast of Florida.
raze	(v.) to demolish or destroyed. e.g. - The continued bombing completely <u>razed</u> the small villages.
reasoned	(adj.) based on good judgement or common sense. e.g. - The judge gave the sentence, providing a <u>reasoned</u> opinion for the judgement. (n.) reason.
rebuke	(v.) to scold or criticize. e.g. - The mother <u>rebuked</u> her child for disobeying her.
rebuff	(v.) to reject or refuse. e.g. - She <u>rebuffed</u> his advances, and told him that they should remain just friends.
receptacle	(n.) a container used for collecting items which are later thrown away. e.g. - All litter should be thrown into the <u>receptacles</u> provided throughout the park.
recess	(v.) to interrupt or suspend an activity or procedure. e.g. - The children are not in class right now. They have <u>recessed</u> for lunch. (n.) recess.
reclusive	(adj.) describing someone who avoids other people, esp. to the point of not being seen in public. e.g. - Howard Hughes led a <u>reclusive</u> life, rarely venturing out in public. (n.) recluse.
rectify	(v.) to make right or correct. e.g. - The bank has promised to <u>rectify</u> the error they made on my account. (n.) rectification; (adj.) rectified.
reform	(v.) to change, esp. to improve sthg. (n.) the act of changing in this way. e.g. - The legal <u>reform</u> will improve the penal system. (adj.) reformed.
refrain (from)	(v.) to restrain or prevent oneself from doing sthg. e.g. - The hospital is a smoke-free zone. That means you must <u>refrain</u> from smoking.
regime	(n.) a strict form of management or government. e.g. - She has a strict exercise <u>regime</u>. She goes to the gym every day.
regress	(v.) to return to an earlier time period. e.g. - Being overwhelmed by the responsibilities of adult life, she wished that she could <u>regress</u> to her childhood. (n.) regression.
rehabilitation	(n.) the action of returning to a state of good health, esp. through the use of therapy. e.g. - After years of alcoholism, she is finally undergoing <u>rehabilitation</u> in order to stop drinking. (v.) rehabilitate; (adj.) rehabilitated.

reiterate	(v.) to repeat or emphasize again. e.g. - The teacher <u>reiterated</u> the instructions to the examination after the student asked a question about them. (n.) reiteration; (adj.) reiterative; (adv.) reiteratively.
rejuvenate	(v.) to make young again, to revive. e.g. - We felt <u>rejuvenated</u> after our vacation. (n.) rejuvenation; (adj.) rejuvenated; rejuvenating.
relegate	(v.) to assign to an inferior group or category. e.g. - The baseball player was <u>relegated</u> to the minor league when he began to play poorly. (n.) relegation.
relinquish	(v.) to surrender or give up. e.g. - The single mother was forced to <u>relinquish</u> her children to the state when she was sentenced to prison. (n.) relinquishment.
reluctant	(adj.) hesitant or unready to act. e.g. - She was <u>reluctant</u> to accept the job when she heard that the salary was quite low. (n.) reluctance; (adv.) reluctantly.
remorse	(n.) the feeling of guilt or sadness about one's own wrongdoings; (syn.) penitence, contrition. e.g. - The murderer showed great <u>remorse</u> for his crimes and asked for the forgiveness of the public. (adj.) remorseful; (adv.) remorsefully.
remunerate	(v.) to pay for a service performed; compensate. e.g. - The company agreed to <u>remunerate</u> me quite highly. My salary will be $20,000 a month. (n.) remuneration; (adj.) remunerated.
render	(v.) to give or provide, esp. a service. e.g. - You must pay the applicable fee for any services <u>rendered</u> to you.
renounce	(v.) to refuse to obey or recognize the authority of. e.g. - Many people who <u>renounced</u> Hitler during World War II were put to death. (n.) renouncement.
renovate	(v.) to renew; to improve the condition of. e.g. - That hotel is currently being <u>renovated</u>. They are repairing the damage caused by the fire. (n.) renovation; (adj.) renovated.
repast	(n.) a meal. e.g. - The soldiers enjoyed their delicious <u>repast</u>, having lived on basic rations for over a week.
repel	(v.) to push back or away. e.g. - This spray <u>repels</u> mosquitoes because the smell is offensive to them. (n.) repulsion, repellent; (adj.) repulsive.
replenish	(v.) to fill sthg up again. e.g. - The supplies need to be <u>replenished</u> every two weeks to avoid running short on any items. (n.) replenishment; (adj.) replenished.

replete (with)	(adj.) complete; abundant. e.g. - The orchestra was replete with all types of wind and string instruments. (n.) repletion.
replicate	(v.) to duplicate or reproduce. e.g. - Cloning may be used in the future to replicate animals. (n.) replication; (adj.) replicated.
reprehensible	(adj.) suitable of receiving great blame or criticism; (syn.) culpable. e.g. - Committing murder is a reprehensible act. (n.) reprehension, reprehensibility; (v.) reprehend; (adv.) reprehensibly.
reprisal	(n.) an act of retaliation. e.g. - Several people died in the reprisals that followed the attack.
reproach	(v.) to give severe criticism or blame; (syn.) rebuke. e.g. - The mother reproached her child for spilling the milk. (n.) reproach; (adj.) reproachful; (adv.) reproachfully.
rescind	(v.) to cancel or evoke. e.g. - They rescinded the purchasing contract upon realizing that he had already sold the item.
residue	(n.) part of sthg which is left over after the main part has been taken away. e.g. - I hate this soap. It leaves a strange residue on my skin that can't be rinsed off. (adj.) residual; (adv.) residually.
resolute	(adj.) acting decisively and with determination. e.g. - He was resolute in his decision to attend college. In fact, he said that nothing could change his mind. (n.) resolve; (v.) resolve; (adv.) resolutely.
respite	(n.) a rest or break, esp. from sthg difficult or unpleasant. e.g. - Spending time with my family on leave was a welcome respite after having been abroad for so many months.
reticent	(adj.) reluctant or unwilling to talk; (syn.) taciturn. e.g. - The suspect was reticent when asked about his participation in the crime.
retract	(v.) to draw back; to withdraw. e.g. - The newspaper retracted the false information that it gave in the article and offered a full apology.
retrospect	(n.) the examination of an event after it has occurred. e.g. - In retrospect, he realizes that it was a mistake to have taken the job. (adj.) retrospective; (adv.) retrospectively.
revile	(v.) to criticize severely; scold; chide; rebuke; (syn.) reproach. e.g. - The newspaper article reviled the government for not providing adequate funding for educational programs.

revival	(n.) the act of making sthg more popular, active, or alive. e.g. - Boxing is enjoying a revival around the country. More people are participating in the sport than ever before. (v.) revive.
rigid	(adj.) strong and unbending. (met.) inflexible or awkward. e.g. - He is such a rigid person. He gets so upset whenever we need to change our plans. (n.) rigidity.
rodent	(n.) a small unwanted animal, such as a rat or a mouse; (syn.) vermin. e.g. - You can set a trap or use poison to deal with rodents in your home.
rudimentary	(adj.) basic or fundamental. e.g. - You will never understand advanced mathematics if you don't learn the rudimentary principles of arithmetic. (n.) rudiment; (adv.) rudimentarily.
ruthless	(adj.) cruel; malicious. e.g. - He is known for especially ruthless crimes against the elderly. (n.) ruthlessness; (adv.) ruthlessly.

Exercises – Q to R

Instructions: Complete the sentences below, using one of the words beginning with the letters "Q" or "R" from the previous section. Note that some gaps may have more than one possible answer. You may also need to change the form of the word. The answers are provided at the end of book.

1) After years of drug addiction, she is finally undergoing _____.

2) The company will begin to _____ the service once you have paid the deposit.

3) The troops were ravenous and thoroughly enjoyed their delicious _____.

4) Those _____ can either be caught with traps or killed with poison.

5) My parents had a few _____ about whether my application was going to be accepted.

6) The president had to _____ control of the company after the merger was complete.

7) That cosmetic is supposed to _____ your skin and make you look ten years younger.

8) He is grouchy all the time and has a reputation for being _____.

9) In _____, he wishes that he had paid better attention in class.

10) I was _____ to lie to the police officer since I knew the punishment for not letting the truth would be severe.

Words – S

Instructions: Study the words below, paying attention to their meanings as well as how they are used in the example sentences. Then complete the exercise that follows.

salvage	(v.) to save sthg, esp. that which has been damaged. e.g. - It was possible to salvage the car after the accident. It is being fixed at the garage right now. (n.) salvage; (adj.) salvageable.
salvo	(n.) the simultaneous discharge of weapons in a battle. e.g. - The battle began with a salvo.
sanctimonious	(adj.) relating to an insincere or hypocritical adherence to high moral standards. e.g. - The wealthy king gave a sanctimonious speech about how money should not be considered the most important thing in life. (n.) sanctimony, sanctimoniousness; (adv.) sanctimoniously.
sanction	(n.) a penalty or punishment for violating a rule or law. (v.) to penalize or punish for such a violation. e.g. - Trade sanctions have been placed upon that country for their refusal to follow global environmental standards. (adj.) sanctioned.
sarcasm	(n.) the act of using language that means the opposite of one intends; (syn.) irony. e.g. - He said it was a beautiful day when it was pouring down with rain. Surely you knew that was sarcasm by the tone of his voice. (adj.) sarcastic.
satire	(n.) the use of humor to ridicule or mock someone. e.g. - Politicians are often the target of satire on humorous television programs that poke fun at them. (adj.) satirical; (adv.) satirically.
saunter	(v.) to walk in an unhurried manner; (syn.) stroll. e.g. - The couple slowly sauntered down the street, looking in the store windows. (n.) saunter.
savory	(adj.) relating to tasty and well-seasoned food. e.g. - They all enjoyed the hot, savory meal. (v.) savor
scald	(v.) to burn with hot water. e.g. - The hot coffee spilled, scalding the baby's skin and causing it to turn red. (adj.) scalding, scalded.
scant	(adj.) a very small amount. e.g. - Due to scant attendance, class was cancelled. (adj.) scanty; (adv.) scantily.
scarlet	(adj.) bright red; (syn.) crimson. e.g. - Her face turned scarlet from being in the sun too long.

scathing	(adj.) harsh; severe; damaging. e.g. - The senator presented a <u>scathing</u> attack on the proposed law. (n.) scathe; (v.) scathe; (adv.) scathingly.
scorch	(v.) to burn with dry heat. e.g. - He <u>scorched</u> the shirt while ironing it, leaving a huge burn on the sleeve. (adj.) scorched.
scrappy	(adj.) prone to fighting and arguing. e.g. - He was a <u>scrappy</u> youth who channeled his aggression by taking up boxing.
scruples	(n.) morals; ethics; standards of behavior. e.g. - People displaying immoral behavior do not have the proper <u>scruples</u>. (adj.) scrupulous; (adv.) scrupulously; (ant.) unscrupulous.
scrutinize	(v.) to examine in great detail. e.g. - He <u>scrutinized</u> the artwork in order to determine if it was authentic. (n.) scrutiny.
scurry	(v.) to hurry; to run in short quick steps. e.g. - The pedestrians <u>scurried</u> for cover when the gunfire broke out.
sedate	(v.) to make calm or quiet, esp. with the use of medication. e.g. - The doctor <u>sedated</u> the patient with tranquilizers. (n.) sedation; (adj.) sedate; (adj.) sedated.
sedulous	(adj.) showing dedication and care. e.g. - The nurse took care of the patient with <u>sedulous</u> attention. (n.) sedulity; (adv.) sedulously
seize	(v.) to take hold of sthg with force or strength. e.g. - The policeman <u>seized</u> the escaped criminal by grabbing him with both arms. (n.) seizure.
semblance	(n.) an outward appearance of sthg, esp. when the reality is different. e.g. - The office showed a <u>semblance</u> of order, but in fact, all of the filing cabinets were full of clutter.
sentry	(n.) a soldier standing guard. e.g. - A <u>sentry</u> was standing guard at the main gate of the army base.
servility	(n.) relating to the behavior of a servant or an individual in an inferior position. e.g. - The employee responded with complete <u>servility</u>, doing whatever his boss demanded. (adj.) servile; (adv.) servilely.
severity	(n.) seriousness. e.g. - The <u>severity</u> of punishment shall be equal to the seriousness of the crime. (adj.) severe; (adv.) severely.
sheaf	(n.) a bundle or collection of sthg. e.g. - A thick <u>sheaf</u> of paper was sitting on top of the desk.

simulate	(v.) to reproduce or copy the appearance of. e.g. - The restaurant tries to simulate the atmosphere from the 1950's. (n.) simulation; (adj.) simulated.
simultaneously	(adv.) at the same time. e.g. - Twins or triplets celebrate their birthdays simultaneously. (n.) simultaneousness, simultaneity; (adj.) simultaneous.
sinecure	(n.) employment for which an individual is paid, but for which no duties or responsibilities are required. e.g. - He is retired now. His job as city clerk is only a sinecure since he doesn't actually work, but still receives a paycheck.
skirmish	(n.) a small fight in a war. e.g. - It was not a full-scale battle, but only a small skirmish.
slander	(v.) to cause damage to an individual's reputation as a result of lying, rumors, or gossip. e.g. - You should not destroy his good name through such slander (n.) slander.
sleek	(adj.) having a smooth, bright surface. e.g. - The new motorcycle had a sleek surface as a result of the bright paint that had been applied to it. (n.) sleekness; (v.) sleek; (adv.) sleekly.
slipshod	(adj.) careless or untidy. e.g. - His work was so slipshod that we had to do it all over again.
slovenly	(adj.) unclean in behavior or appearance. e.g. - He looked slovenly in his dirty shoes and torn jeans.
snag	(n.) problem or difficulty; (syn.) snafu. e.g. - We experienced several snags on our vacation, including being robbed and losing our luggage. (v.) snag.
snare	(n.) a small trap for animals (v.) to trap an animal in such a device. (met.) to lure or tempt someone. e.g. - The predators snared their innocent victims by asking them for directions and then abducting them.
sneaky	(adj.) relating to an individual who uses dishonesty or exploitation; sly; (syn.) cunning. e.g. - It was very sneaky of him to steal money from the people who had grown to trust him. (n.) sneak; (v.) sneak.
sodden	(adj.) waterlogged; (syn.) boggy. e.g. - Our boots were sodden after marching across the swamp.
solace	(n.) comfort in time of great sadness; (syn.) succor. e.g. - We hope you will find solace in the fact that your daughter died while defending the lives of others. (v.) console.

solicit	(v.) to request; to attempt to acquire or obtain. e.g. - After being charged with murder, he <u>solicited</u> the advice of a lawyer. (n.) solicitation.
solvent	(adj.) in a good financial condition; not bankrupt. e.g. - The company was <u>solvent</u> because it had over one million dollars in the bank. (n.) solvency.
somber	(adj.) gloomy or depressing. e.g. - The atmosphere at the funeral was made more <u>somber</u> by the rain and dark clouds.
spawn	(v.) to produce or cause to develop; to create. e.g. - His argumentative attitude often <u>spawns</u> many disagreements. (n.) spawn.
specimen	(n.) a sample, esp. one used for purposes of examination. e.g. - The doctor took a blood <u>specimen</u> from my arm in order to determine the cause of my illness.
spectator	(n.) a person who watches or observes sthg. e.g. - There were many <u>spectators</u> watching the football game. (v.) spectate.
spontaneous	(adj.) describing sthg unplanned or done on the spur of the moment; (syn.) impromptu. e.g. - The crowd broke into <u>spontaneous</u> cheers when their team made a touchdown. (n.) spontaneity; (adv.) spontaneously.
squalor	(n.) the state of being filthy and neglected. e.g. - Many houses in the poor, run-down neighborhood exist in a state of <u>squalor</u>. (adj.) squalid.
stagnant	(adj.) not moving; standing still. e.g. - The water in this lake is <u>stagnant</u> since it doesn't flow to another waterway. (n.) stagnation; (v.) stagnate; (adv.) stagnantly.
stalwart	(adj.) strong, reliable, and loyal. (n.) a stalwart person. e.g. - He is a <u>stalwart</u> supporter of the Republican party.
staunch	(adj.) relating to strength in one's beliefs or opinions. e.g. - He is a <u>staunch</u> supporter of that charity and often donates money to their causes. (adv.) staunchly.
stifle	(v.) to suppress, discourage, or hold back. e.g. - Why do you always <u>stifle</u> me when I want to speak? I have the right to express my opinions.
stipulate	(v.) to specify sthg as part of an agreement. e.g. - The restraining order <u>stipulated</u> that the two people were not to attempt to communicate with each other in any way. (n.) stipulation; (adj.) stipulated.

strenuous	(adj.) demanding great physical strength or endurance. e.g. - Lifting the heavy box was a very strenuous task. (adv.) strenuously.
strewn	(adj.) spread; scattered; thrown around. e.g. - His bedroom was a mess. Everything was strewn about. (v.) strew.
strident	(adj.) hoarse; (syn.) grating. e.g. - Many people find the sound of her strident voice to be irritating.
strife	(n.) conflict; friction. e.g. - There is a good deal of strife in Congress. Politicians are always arguing about differing viewpoints.
stringent	(adj.) strict or rigid. e.g. - Bruce's father has many stringent rules and often punishes him. (adv.) stringently.
studious	(adj.) relating to individuals who read or study extensively. e.g. - She is very studious. She spends five hours a day doing her homework.
stupendous	(adj.) amazing or astounding in size. e.g. - The circus was stupendous. It included one hundred different kinds of animals. (adv.) stupendously.
sturdy	(adj.) relating to objects that are strong and solid. e.g. - This table is sturdy and can hold quite heavy objects. (adv.) sturdily.
subdued	(adj.) to control or reduce in degree of feeling. e.g. - She was quite angry earlier in the week, but she's feeling more subdued now.
subject (to)	(v.) to force to experience or endure sthg, esp. sthg unpleasant or unwanted. e.g. - He was subjected to punishment from his father for arriving home late.
subjugate	(v.) to suppress or take control of. e.g. - The police attempted to subjugate the rioters. (n.) subjugation.
sublime	(adj.) relating to sthg that is extremely excellent, awesome, or beautiful. e.g. - The tourists enjoyed the sublime sight of the Grand Canyon. (n.) sublimity; (adv.) sublimely.
submerge	(v.) to place an object under the surface of the water. e.g. - Katie frightened us when she submerged herself in the lake for three minutes. We were worried that she might have drowned. (n.) submergence.
subordinate	(adj.) being less in rank or authority. e.g. - He has a subordinate position in the company. There are ten managers in authority over him. (n.) subordination, subordinate; (v.) subordinate.

subsequent	(adj.) following in sequence, order, or time. e.g. - Subsequent to high school, she decided to enlist. (adv.) subsequently.
subside	(v.) to settle downwards. e.g. - The ground subsided during the earthquake. Geologists now estimate that it is three inches lower than before. (n.) subsidence.
subsistence	(n.) the minimum amount of food necessary for human existence. e.g. - Children in certain countries in Africa do not have enough food for normal subsistence. Some of them are starving. (v.) subsist.
subterfuge	(n.) trickery used in order free oneself from blame or responsibility. e.g. - The suspect's subterfuge consisted of telling the police that his identical twin brother had committed the crime.
succulent	(adj.) relating to food that is juicy and moist. e.g. - He had to wash his hands after eating the juicy, succulent pear. (n.) succulence; (adv.) succulently.
sumptuous	(adj.) extremely rich in texture or quality. e.g. - The queen's palace had sumptuous decorations. (n.) sumptuousness; (adv.) sumptuously.
supercilious	(adj.) arrogant; conceited. e.g. - He is the most supercilious person I know. He thinks he knows everything about everything. (n.) superciliousness; (adv.) superciliously.
superficial	(adj.) not deep or profound; surface. e.g. - She is a superficial woman. Her only interests are clothes and make-up. (adv.) superficially.
superfluous	(adj.) beyond what is necessary. e.g. - The teacher asked for a three-hundred word composition. Writing a thousand words was totally superfluous. (n.) superfluity; (adv.) superfluously.
supersede	(v.) to cause to become outdated as a result of being replaced; to become deprecated; (syn.) supplant. e.g. - That law is no longer effective as it has been superseded by a new law. (n.) supersession.
superstition	(n.) a belief in supernatural powers or occurrences. e.g. - She believed in the superstition that black cats cause bad luck. (adj.) superstitious; (adv.) superstitiously.
supplicate	(v.) to beg, plead, or grovel; (syn.) entreat. e.g. - The prisoners supplicated the men in the firing squad to spare their lives. (n.) supplication. (n.) supplicant; (adj.) supplicatory.

suppress	(v.) to cause to stop or prevent for a period of time. e.g. - This syrup will suppress your cough for three hours. (n.) suppression, suppressant; (adj.) suppressed.
surmount	(v.) to overcome sthg, esp. a difficulty or problem. e.g. - The businessman finally surmounted his cash flow problem by getting a loan form the bank. (adj.) surmountable.
surplus	(n.) an excessive quantity, beyond what is required or necessary. e.g. - The army had a surplus of boots, which were stored in a warehouse.
susceptible	(adj.) describing the state of being prone or vulnerable to sthg. e.g. - She has just been released from an addiction program, so she might be susceptible to a relapse. (n.) susceptibility; (adv.) susceptibly.
sustenance	(n.) food; nourishment. e.g. - Healthy food and clean water are necessary for human sustenance. (v.) sustain.
sycophantic	(adj.) relating to using excessive flattery to gain someone's favor. e.g. - He is one of the most sycophantic people I know. He is always giving her compliments to butter her up. (n.) sycophant.

Exercises – S

Instructions: Complete the sentences below, using one of the words beginning with the letter "S" from the previous section. Note that some gaps may have more than one possible answer. You may also need to change the form of the word. The answers are provided at the end of book.

1) The surgeon performed the operation with _____ care and attention.

2) His job with the company is a _____ because he doesn't do any real work for the money.

3) That water is _____. It is not fit to drink and is beginning to smell bad.

4) The carpenter's work was so _____ that the cupboard he built for us collapsed after we had it for only a week.

5) You will appear _____ if you never clean your shoes or comb your hair.

6) The barn was in a state of _____ because the manure hadn't been taken away for months.

7) The anti-gravity capsule attempts to _____ flight in outer space.

8) Carrying two hundred pounds of luggage through three airports was certainly a _____ task.

9) The political party leader is so _____. He is really corrupt, but he always talks about the importance of being honest.

10) There was a great deal of artillery fire in the _____.

Words – T

Instructions: Study the words below, paying attention to their meanings as well as how they are used in the example sentences. Then complete the exercise that follows.

tactful	(adj.) sensitive in dealing with difficult issues; diplomatic. e.g. - They were too <u>tactful</u> to say anything negative. (n.) tact; tactfulness; (adv.) tactfully.
tangible	(adj.) being perceived by the senses; real; material. e.g. - The insensitive man valued his <u>tangible</u> possessions more than love or friendship. (n.) tangibility; (adv.) tangibly. (ant.) intangible
tantamount (to)	(adj.) equal to in terms of results or consequences. e.g. - Refusing to tell the entire truth is <u>tantamount</u> to lying.
tardiness	(n.) lateness for school or work. e.g. - His <u>tardiness</u> at work has become a serious problem. He was warned that he will be fired the next time he's late. (adj.) tardy.
taut	(adj.) tight or tense. e.g. - We need to pull the rope <u>taut</u> to secure the load.
tedious	(adj.) monotonous or tiring. e.g. - Working in a factory assembly line is <u>tedious</u> work. Most factory workers suffer from boredom. (n.) tedium; (adv.) tediously.
temperamental	(adj.) excessively sensitive or unpredictable in mood or state of mind; (syn.) peevish. e.g. - He is so <u>temperamental</u> that you never know what kind of mood he will be in. (n.) temperament; (adv.) temperamentally.
temporal	(adj.) relating to the present time or to worldly phenomena or needs. e.g. - Monks are required to place little importance on <u>temporal</u> needs, such as food and clothing, in order to concentrate on spiritual concerns. (n.) temporality; (adv.) temporally.
tenet	(n.) belief; doctrine; dogma. e.g. - One of the basic <u>tenets</u> of mathematics is that any unknown quantity can be calculated by using the proper equation.
terminate	(v.) to end sthg. e.g. - San Diego is the last stop on our journey, so the trip <u>terminates</u> here. (n.) termination; (adj.) terminated.
terse	(adj.) unnecessarily brief or abrupt in speech. e.g. - Mia was so <u>terse</u> this morning. When I asked her how she was, she told me that is was none of my business. (n.) terseness; (adv.) tersely.

testament	(n.) written proof relating to the disposal of property after an individual's death. e.g. - An individual's last will and testament is often read after the funeral in order to determine how property should be distributed.
testify	(v.) to make a statement in court under oath. e.g. - Brittney witnessed the bank robbery and must testify in court about what she saw take place. (n.) testimony; (n.) testimonial.
thrift	(n.) the act of watching one's spending closely. e.g. - We will need to encourage the habit of thrift since we will have limited money and resources. (adj.) thrifty; (adv.) thriftily.
throng	(n.) a crowd or large gathering of people. e.g. - A noisy throng of spectators was present at the basketball championship. (v.) throng.
thwart	(v.) to oppose, prevent, hinder, or frustrate. e.g. - His poor health thwarted his progress in school.
tolerate	(v.) to possess the ability to accept or endure another person's behavior, esp. when it is offensive or undesirable. e.g. - I don't really enjoy his company, but I can tolerate him sometimes.
transpose	(v.) to exchange or transfer places. e.g. - The figures did not add up because she had transposed some of the numbers in the list. (n.) transposition; (adj.) transposed.
treacherous	(adj.) dangerous or untrustworthy; (syn.) precarious. e.g. - The weather is treacherous today. Travel is not advised. (n.) treacherousness, treachery; (adv.) treacherously.
treason	(n.) the action of disloyalty or betrayal towards an individual's government of nationality or citizenship. e.g. - The officer was accused of treason for revealing military secrets.
treaty	(n.) an agreement made between or among two or more nations. e.g. - An import/export treaty exists between the U.S. and Japan.
tributary	(n.) a river which enters a larger river or lake. e.g. - The Missouri River is a tributary of the Mississippi River as it flows into the Mississippi at St. Louis.
trite	(adj.) relating to a comment that is obvious and overused; (syn.) banal. e.g. - Saying that my mother was "in a better place" when she died was a really trite comment. (n.) triteness; (adv.) tritely.
truncate	(v.) to shorten or cut off, esp. unintentionally. e.g. - The document was truncated went you sent it by email. We only received the first two pages. (n.) truncation; (adj.) truncated.

trying	(adj.) physically, mentally, or psychologically demanding; (syn.) arduous; enervating. e.g. - She finds her boss's complaints and demands very trying.
turbulent	(adj.) causing the development of violence or disturbance. e.g. - The turbulent atmosphere in the city is a result of disharmony among various races. (n.) turbulence.
turmoil	(n.) a state of confusion or disturbance; (syn.) upheaval. e.g. - The country was in turmoil after years of civil war.

Exercises – T

Instructions: Complete the sentences below, using one of the words beginning with the letter "T" from the previous section. Note that some gaps may have more than one possible answer. You may also need to change the form of the word. The answers are provided at the end of book.

1) You have to _____ in court if you see a crime take place.

2) Her job is difficult and _____. She has thought about quitting many times.

3) One of the basic _____ of being a businessperson is that sometimes you have to spend money in order to make money.

4) The ten-page report was _____. We received only the first page.

5) Saying that you aren't that fond of her is _____ to saying that you really don't like her.

6) His house and car were the _____ indications of his success in life.

7) _____ for class will not be tolerated. Students will have to report to the principal if they are late to class.

8) Our progress in setting up camp was _____ by the poor weather.

9) I can't get any information or help from my supervisor. When I try to speak with her, she only gives me very _____ responses.

10) A loud _____ of one thousand people started the protest.

Words – U to V

Instructions: Study the words below, paying attention to their meanings as well as how they are used in the example sentences. Then complete the exercise that follows.

ultimatum	(n.) the action of being presented with two difficult or undesirable choices. e.g. - The student received the ultimatum that he would be expelled if his grades did not improve.
unanimous	(adj.) relating to full and total agreement by all members of a group. e.g. - The new law received the unanimous support of all members of Congress. (n.) unanimity; (adv.) unanimously.
unblemished	(adj.) faultless or pure. e.g. - Even an unfounded, minor charge can damage a person with an unblemished reputation.
unconventional	(adj.) non-traditional; very unusual or eccentric. e.g. - She is a very unconventional woman. She has many unusual habits. (adv.) unconventionally.
undaunted	(adj.) courageous; not afraid or discouraged by opposition or adversity. e.g. - The pilot was undaunted, in spite of the danger he faced. (v.) daunt.
undermine	(v.) to weaken gradually. e.g. - His health was undermined by the progression of the disease. (adj.) undermined.
undertaking	(n.) a project, enterprise, or job, especially one of significant size or effort. e.g. - Painting a fifteen-room house in a day was a huge undertaking. (n.) undertake.
unsavory	(adj.) distasteful; (syn.) insipid. e.g. - This soup is unsavory and isn't fit to eat. (ant.) savory.
unscathed	(adj.) unharmed. e.g. - Although the tornado passed through the town, her house remained unscathed.
unscrupulous	(adj.) without honest or integrity. e.g. - She lost all her money in an unscrupulous business arrangement. (n.) unscrupulousness; (adv.) unscrupulously.
unwavering	(adj.) constant; unchanging. e.g. - He has always been a football fanatic. His enthusiasm for the sport is unwavering.
unilateral	(adj.) one-sided. e.g. - His decision was completely unilateral since no one else agreed to do it.
upheaval	(n.) the action of causing tumult, disturbance, or disorder. e.g. - He always causes upheaval in the class with his constant interruptions.

utilize	(v.) to use with practical effect. e.g. - We will need to utilize an effective strategy if we want to beat our opponent. (n.) utilization; (adj.) utilizable.
utmost	(adj.) the highest or greatest aspect of sthg. e.g. - Brushing your teeth daily is of the utmost importance for good dental hygiene.
vacate	(v.) to leave and no longer occupy a particular place. e.g. - You will need to vacate the hotel room by noon so that it can be used by the next guest.
vacillate	(v.) to waver back and forth between alternative choices. e.g. - She continued to vacillate between the two choices and was unable to make a decision. (n.) vacillation; (adj.) vacillated, vacillating; (adv.) vacillatingly.
vagrant	(n.) a person who does not have a fixed place of residence; a homeless person; (syn.) transient. e.g. - The homeless shelter is full of needy vagrants at this time of year. (n.) vagrancy; (adj.) vagrant.
valiantly	(adv.) being done with strength, bravery, and determination; heroically. e.g. - The firefighter died valiantly in the blaze, saving the life of a small child. (adj.) valiant.
vanquish	(v.) to defeat entirely; (syn.) trounce. e.g. - We vanquished the enemy through our effective strategy.
ventilation	(n.) the action of receiving sufficient air or oxygen. e.g.- The window was opened so that the room could receive some ventilation. (v.) ventilate; (adj.) ventilated.
venture	(n.) a business arrangement involving risk or speculation. e.g. - Gambling at Las Vegas can be a dangerous venture.
venue	(n.) the place or location at which an event takes place. e.g. - The stadium is the venue for the concert.
verbose	(adj.) excessively wordy. e.g. - Everyone had a hard time understanding her verbose instructions. (n.) verbosity; (adv.) verbosely.
verdict	(n.) decision by a jury in court. e.g. - If the jury returns a verdict of guilty at the end of a trial, the suspect will be sent to prison.
verify	(v.) to determine the truth of. e.g. - A lie detector test is often used to verify the details of statements given by suspects. (n.) verification, verity; veracity (adj.) verified.
versatile	(adj.) possessing many skills, talents, or uses. e.g. - My niece is a very versatile musician. She knows how to play the piano and guitar and can also sing beautifully. (n.) versatility.

vessel	(n.) a ship or boat. e.g. - He owns an expensive sailboat. It is really an amazing vessel and has the most modern equipment.
vestibule	(n.) a sheltered or enclosed entrance to a particular place. e.g. - They were collecting donations for charity in the vestibule of the superstore.
vicarious	(adj.) lived or experienced through the actions of others. e.g. - My mother gets vicarious enjoyment by seeing me go to college since she never had the chance to further her education. (n.) vicariousness; (adv.) vicariously.
vicious	(adj.) relating to the desire to cause harm or injury; cruel. e.g. - The lies you said about me were vicious. You only wanted to hurt me. (n.) viciousness; (adv.) viciously.
vicissitude	(n.) a change in a situation or circumstance, generally for the worse. e.g. - There have been many vicissitudes in the economy this year, including a rise in unemployment and an increase in the rate of inflation.
victuals	(n.)(also vittles) food. e.g. - Our victuals are stored in the refrigerator and kitchen cupboards.
vie	(v.) to engage in competition or rivalry. e.g. - The two teams will vie for the championship on Sunday.
vigilant	(adj.) exercising extreme care or caution in outlook. e.g. - The doctors were vigilant in watching the President after his heart attack. (n.) vigilance; (adv.) vigilantly.
villain	(n.) dishonest person; criminal; crook. e.g. - The villain cheated the elderly couple out of their life savings. (v.) vilify.
vindication	(n.) the action of seeking revenge or setting free from blame. e.g. - His vindication from the charge of murder came when the judge announced that he was not guilty. (v.) vindicate.
vindictive	(adj.) having a strong, unreasonable desire for revenge. e.g. - Criticizing a person in a wheelchair for not being able to walk is vindictive and unreasonable. (n.) vindictiveness; (adv.) vindictively.
violation	(n.) offense; crime. e.g. - It is a violation of traffic laws to drive a car after dark without turning its lights on. (v.) violate.
virile	(adj.) the quality of being full of strength and energy. e.g. - The virile weight-lifter managed to lift seven hundred pounds.
viscous	(adj.) thick or sticky. e.g. - Motor oil is an extremely viscous substance. (n.) viscosity.

vital	(adj.) very important or necessary. e.g. - Studying is vital if you want to do well on your examinations. (adv.) vitally.
vocational	(adj.) relating to training or education in a particular skill or craft. e.g. - The college offers many vocational courses, including woodworking and automotive repair. (n.) vocation.
vociferous	(adj.) expressing intense or forceful feelings or emotions. e.g. - Her hatred of the opposing party was clear in the vociferous opinions she expressed. (n.) vociferousness; (adv.) vociferously.
voracious	(adj.) very hungry or eager. e.g. - We had better have enough food because he always has a voracious appetite. (n.) voraciousness, voracity; (adv.) voraciously.
voluble	(adj.) very talkative. e.g. - My best friend is so voluble that she is almost always talking.
voluntarily	(adv.) being done by free choice, without external pressure or influence. e.g. - My neighbor works at the local hospital voluntarily three times a week, even though he receives no payment for his services. (n.) volunteer; (v.) volunteer; (adj.) voluntary.
vulgar	(adj.) offensive in content or expression; lewd; in bad taste. e.g. - Many CDs have warnings because their songs contain vulgar lyrics. (n.) vulgarity.

Exercises – U to V

Instructions: Complete the sentences below, using one of the words beginning with the letters "U" to "V" from the previous section. Note that some gaps may have more than one possible answer. You may also need to change the form of the word. The answers are provided at the end of book.

1) He _____ between two versions of the story, so it was impossible to tell which one was true.

2) The progress of the construction of the building was _____ by the poor weather.

3) If the jury returns a _____ of innocent, the suspect will be released.

4) Adopting a child is an incredible _____. So much responsibility is involved in raising a child.

5) The management of that company is very _____. I have never heard of any other company that permits employees to sleep on the job.

6) The auditorium is the _____ for the graduation ceremony.

7) _____ in the economy have caused many companies to go out of business in recent years.

8) I gave my son the _____ that he would have to leave home if he continued to shoplift.

9) Her love for her children is _____. Nothing could change her feelings.

10) Using profanity, swearing, and spitting are _____ habits.

Words W to Z

Instructions: Study the words below, paying attention to their meanings as well as how they are used in the example sentences. Then complete the exercise that follows.

wary	(adj.) cautious because of concerns or worries about sthg, esp. about safety. e.g. - He was very wary of traveling through such a bad neighborhood. (n.) wariness; (adv.) warily.
wayward	(adj.) being done contrary to the expectations of society or others. e.g. - She was a wayward adolescent. She helped rob a bank when she was just thirteen.
weal	(n.) well-being. e.g. - All cadets will be provided with nutritious meals during training to ensure the common weal.
weary	(adj.) very tired. e.g. - The trip lasted thirty-two hours and the travelers were quite weary from the journey. (adv.) wearily.
whim	(n.) a sudden or eccentric idea or impulse. e.g. - She dyed her hair bright purple on a whim. (adj.) whimsical.
wholesome	(adj.) acceptable in terms of health, character, or morals; (syn.) salubrious, salutary. e.g. - Milk is a wholesome drink because it is full of vitamins and minerals. (n.) wholesomeness.
winded	(adj.) out of breath. e.g. - The recruits were winded after doing the basic training exercises. (v.) wind.
winsome	(adj.) charming; pleasant; cheerful; (syn.) affable, amiable, cordial. e.g. - Jane is a very winsome girl. She is rarely unhappy.
wistful	(adj.) causing sadness or depression. e.g. - Alison felt wistful when she lost her job, and she went into a deep depression. (adv.) wistfully.
wither	(v.) to lack freshness as a result of becoming dried out. e.g. - If you don't put those flowers in some water, they will wither. (adj.) withered.
wrath	(n.) anger. e.g. - You will suffer the wrath of your parents if you disobey them.
wretched	(adj.) being particularly bad in quality; (syn.) dismal. e.g. - The team's performance was wretched and, of course, they lost the game. (n.) wretchedness; (adv.) wretchedly.
wry	(adj.) relating to matter-of-fact humor; (syn.) droll. e.g. - Her wry comments made all of us laugh. (n.) wryness; (adv.) wryly.

yearn	(v.) to crave or desire. e.g. - Having grown tired of city life, William yearned for a life in the country. (n.) yearning.
zealot	(n.) an individual displaying unreasonable enthusiasm; fanatic. e.g. - Susan is an absolute zealot about her exercise routine. She goes to the gym twice a day. (adj.) zealous; (adv.) zealously.
zest	(n.) enthusiasm and energy. e.g. - I attempted to beat my past record by running the race with zest. (adj.) zestful; zesty; (adv.) zestfully.

Exercises – W to Z

Instructions: Complete the sentences below, using one of the words beginning with the letters "W" to "Z" from the previous section. Note that some gaps may have more than one possible answer. You may also need to change the form of the word. The answers are provided at the end of book.

1) He was _____ of beginning the journey when it was raining so heavily.

2) She is a _____ about keeping the house clean. She cleans it every day.

3) These fresh herbs will _____ if it is too hot in the kitchen.

4) I felt absolutely _____ yesterday. I couldn't even get out of bed.

5) The color of his skin indicated his good health and _____ .

6) He started the job with _____, but soon got tired and lost his enthusiasm.

7) John's _____ sense of humor always makes everyone laugh.

8) Having been away from home for a year, she _____ to see her family.

9) She was so _____ when she moved and had to say goodbye to all her good friends.

10) Those who fail to follow social norms will suffer the _____ of society.

ASVAB WORD KNOWLEDGE – PRACTICE TEST 1

You should allow yourself 11 minutes to complete each practice test in order to simulate the actual exam.

1. Farming and raising animals are important for the domestic economy.
   A. state
   B. national
   C. county
   D. annual

2. The child was gnawing his candy.
   A. sucking
   B. eating
   C. chewing
   D. swallowing

3. There have been some pervasive changes to the school's curriculum.
   A. extensive
   B. admirable
   C. difficult
   D. approved

4. It is often said that a person can be conspicuous by his or her absence.
   A. unaware
   B. acknowledged
   C. concealed
   D. noticeable

5. She said she didn't have the inclination to go out tonight.
   A. money
   B. desire
   C. time
   D. availability

6. No matter what we said, he was impervious to our suggestions.
   A. humiliated by
   B. critical of
   C. incapable of
   D. unaffected by

7. Traveling on that winding road into town is treacherous.
   A. dangerous
   B. ill-advised
   C. exciting
   D. tiring

8. The court case is surrounded by a(n) labyrinth of counterclaims.
   A. excess
   B. abundance
   C. maze
   D. puzzle

9. Elderly people are often prone to broken bones.
   A. troubled by
   B. vulnerable to
   C. afraid of
   D. overwhelmed by

10. The criminal had no contrition for his crimes.
    A. verdict
    B. punishment
    C. confession
    D. remorse

11. She had superficial injuries from the accident.
    A. ugly
    B. unexpected
    C. bloody
    D. slight

12. He will spend twenty years in prison for his involvement in illicit activities.
    A. unlawful
    B. imprudent
    C. shameful
    D. harmful

13. He has had a(n) illustrious career in the military.
    A. respectful
    B. outstanding
    C. elusive
    D. earnest

14. She needs to surmount her problems in order to get ahead in life.
    A. learn from
    B. endure
    C. overcome
    D. forget

15. Our lack of money is no obstacle towards finishing the project.
    A. facilitation
    B. assistance
    C. significance
    D. hindrance

16. He is a(n) layperson on that subject.
    A. amateur
    B. expert
    C. disinterested party
    D. academic

17. In order to be a good parent, one must foster a caring attitude.
    A. display
    B. adopt
    C. demonstrate
    D. present

18. Consensus most nearly means:
    A. discussion
    B. unanimity
    C. agreement
    D. harmony

19. Jeopardy most nearly means:
    A. chance
    B. danger
    C. insecurity
    D. unprotected

20. Elaborate most nearly means:
    A. unusual
    B. artificial
    C. invented
    D. extensive

21. Abate most nearly means:
    A. lessen
    B. lighten
    C. relinquish
    D. subdue

22. Sublime most nearly means:
    A. sensitive
    B. unforgettable
    C. excessive
    D. wonderful

23. Pithy most nearly means:
    A. absurd
    B. bitter
    C. brief
    D. weak

24. Livid most nearly means:
    A. upset
    B. furious
    C. annoyed
    D. emotional

25. Ruthless most nearly means:
    A. terrible
    B. obnoxious
    C. unkind
    D. cruel

26. Supplicate most nearly means:
    A. beg
    B. complain
    C. ask
    D. communicate

27. Abscond most nearly means:
    A. rob
    B. blackmail
    C. avoid capture
    D. dissipate

28. Paradox most nearly means:
    A. ambiguity
    B. enigma
    C. riddle
    D. contradiction

29. Subordinate most nearly means:
    A. unequal
    B. junior
    C. minor
    D. unnecessary

30. Fathom most nearly means:
    A. comprehend
    B. complicate
    C. recognize
    D. assess

31. Burnished most nearly means:
    A. waxed
    B. on fire
    C. polished
    D. engraved

32. Contaminate most nearly means:
    A. dump
    B. pollute
    C. harm
    D. filthy

33. Intrepid most nearly means:
    A. steadfast
    B. ambulatory
    C. adventurous
    D. fearless

34. Predilection most nearly means:
    A. preference
    B. perversion
    C. benediction
    D. antipathy

35. Semblance most nearly means:
    A. approximation
    B. attitude
    C. appearance
    D. awareness

ASVAB WORD KNOWLEDGE – PRACTICE TEST 2

1. I wouldn't keep company with a(n) unsavory character like him.
   A. domineering
   B. awkward
   C. distasteful
   D. overbearing

2. The situation was fraught with stress and tension.
   A. full
   B. obvious
   C. plain
   D. clandestine

3. His day was filled with mundane tasks.
   A. frivolous
   B. obsequious
   C. interesting
   D. ordinary

4. Pandemic most nearly means:
   A. illness
   B. infection
   C. incidence
   D. outbreak

5. The two counties are contiguous.
   A. catching
   B. adjoining
   C. infectious
   D. cordial

6. The newspaper article reviled the new law.
   A. renewed
   B. reappraised
   C. evaluated
   D. criticized

7. Supercilious most nearly means:
   A. conceited
   B. ridiculous
   C. impervious
   D. ridiculed

8. We need to keep the rope taut.
   A. coiled
   B. tense
   C. submerged
   D. level

9. He went to Hollywood on a(n) whim.
   A. trip
   B. desire
   C. impulse
   D. jaunt

10. He has several lucrative businesses.
    A. consolidated
    B. financial
    C. time-consuming
    D. profitable

11. Opulent most nearly means:
    A. luxurious
    B. palatial
    C. expensive
    D. decadent

12. Inamorata most nearly means:
    A. boyfriend
    B. girlfriend
    C. spouse
    D. husband

13. A(n) treaty exists between the United States and the United Kingdom.
    A. boycott
    B. contract
    C. treatise
    D. agreement

14. This suitcase is very sturdy and should last a long time.
    A. heavy
    B. useful
    C. strong
    D. inimical

15. Rancid most nearly means:
    A. putrid
    B. unpleasant
    C. impure
    D. rampant

16. Maria was caught in a sudden deluge.
    A. downpour
    B. ambush
    C. storm
    D. crevice

17. This is a portrait of an eminent politician.
    A. disreputable
    B. distinguished
    C. impending
    D. forthcoming

18. He gave us a(n) eloquent speech at the ceremony.
    A. grandiose
    B. wordy
    C. staunch
    D. articulate

19. Fallible most nearly means:
    A. foolproof
    B. unacceptable
    C. errant
    D. diminished

20. There is rapport between the two countries.
    A. treaty
    B. harmony
    C. embargo
    D. communication

21. Embonpoint most nearly means:
    A. plumpness
    B. revealed
    C. attacked
    D. elegant

22. All of the passengers perished.
    A. waited
    B. disappeared
    C. boarded
    D. died

23. Impartial most nearly means:
    A. equanimity
    B. magnanimity
    C. fair
    D. biased

24. We have been asked to peruse the statue.
    A. interpret   C. assess
    B. read   D. file

25. Vital most nearly means the opposite of:
    A. unnecessary   C. lively
    B. sentient   D. essential

26. Conducive most nearly means:
    A. beneficial   C. circuitous
    B. electrical   D. regulated

27. Elite most nearly means:
    A. ludicrous   C. enlightened
    B. exclusive   D. costly

28. Barrier most nearly means:
    A. gateway   C. impediment
    B. crossroads   D. enforcement

29. Overtone most nearly means:
    A. proposition   C. advancement
    B. invitation   D. suggestion

30. Sumptuous most nearly means:
    A. audacious   C. substantial
    B. pretentious   D. luxurious

31. Indelible most nearly means the opposite of:
    A. unforgettable   C. tasteless
    B. spoiled   D. impermanent

32. Aghast most nearly means:
    A. undaunted   C. apprehensive
    B. appalled   D. unsurprised

33. Conflagration most nearly means:
    A. beating   C. inferno
    B. flailing   D. mishap

34. Barrage most nearly means:
    A. vessel   C. bombardment
    B. initiative   D. artillery

35. Fecund most nearly means:
    A. luscious   C. infertile
    B. favorable   D. productive

ASVAB WORD KNOWLEDGE – PRACTICE TEST 3

1. Their company <u>fabricates</u> wooden sheds.
   A. designs
   B. assembles
   C. dismantles
   D. exports

2. Please put it in the <u>receptacle</u> when you are finished.
   A. appliance
   B. display
   C. wastebasket
   D. mailbox

3. Students should learn the <u>rudimentary</u> aspects of English grammar.
   A. fundamental
   B. advanced
   C. important
   D. problematic

4. He was a <u>scrappy</u> youngster.
   A. orphaned
   B. small
   C. poorly-dressed
   D. aggressive

5. He was told that the message was <u>imperative</u>.
   A. calamitous
   B. verbose
   C. indecipherable
   D. urgent

6. The specific details of the plan remained <u>covert</u> to the group.
   A. undisclosed
   B. loquacious
   C. terse
   D. private

7. Tony was a <u>precocious</u> child.
   A. unruly
   B. talented
   C. outspoken
   D. magnanimous

8. Her problems were <u>insurmountable</u>.
   A. pervasive
   B. troublesome
   C. insuperable
   D. exaggerated

9. The building was <u>razed</u> in three days.
   A. occupied
   B. finished
   C. constructed
   D. demolished

10. His <u>countenance</u> seemed to indicate that he was depressed.
    A. expression
    B. mood
    C. posture
    D. temperament

11. He has such a strange <u>appellation</u>.
    A. habit
    B. name
    C. quirk
    D. appearance

12. She was convicted of perjury.
    A. lying
    B. stealing
    C. perfidy
    D. contempt

13. Inventing the new machine involved a(n) immense amount of research and development.
    A. assiduous
    B. duplicitous
    C. indigent
    D. enormous

14. The hospital has recently received a(n) endowment.
    A. faculty
    B. gift
    C. resource
    D. loan

15. Darren is quite deft at using the computer.
    A. unskilled
    B. adept
    C. educated
    D. cogent

16. He is facing a predicament right now.
    A. dilemma
    B. obstacle
    C. inquiry
    D. decision

17. He has contended with many problems in his life.
    A. ignored
    B. procured
    C. managed
    D. brought on

18. The store was inundated with customers.
    A. overwhelmed by
    B. occupied by
    C. lacking in
    D. dealing with

19. Maladroit most nearly means:
    A. evil
    B. villainous
    C. difficult
    D. clumsy

20. Immerse most nearly means:
    A. dampen
    B. plunge
    C. extensive
    D. colossal

21. Sanction most nearly means:
    A. purge
    B. punish
    C. approve
    D. endorse

22. Feasible most nearly means:
    A. inappropriate
    B. impractical
    C. achievable
    D. trustworthy

23. Vanquish most nearly means:
    A. cleanse
    B. remove
    C. defeat
    D. demolish

24. Complacent most nearly means:
    A. self-satisfied
    B. forgetful
    C. exhausted
    D. lazy

25. Detrimental most nearly means:
    A. pointless
    B. unhealthy
    C. heedless
    D. harmful

26. Compendious most nearly means:
    A. capable
    B. comprehensive
    C. pendent
    D. published

27. Dwindle most nearly means:
    A. arise
    B. descend
    C. enhance
    D. diminish

28. Florescent most nearly means:
    A. alight
    B. glowing
    C. flowering
    D. growing

29. Canny most nearly means:
    A. shrewd
    B. alike
    C. frightening
    D. surprising

30. Accost most nearly means:
    A. detain
    B. attack
    C. imprison
    D. torture

31. Savory most nearly means:
    A. edible
    B. warm
    C. heated
    D. tasty

32. Larceny most nearly means:
    A. theft
    B. deception
    C. shoplifting
    D. criminal

33. Illusion most nearly means:
    A. implication
    B. viewpoint
    C. misapprehension
    D. day dream

34. Lethargic most nearly means:
    A. inattentive
    B. sluggish
    C. laid-back
    D. introverted

35. Novice most nearly means:
    A. non-expert
    B. trainee
    C. cadet
    D. beginner

ASVAB WORD KNOWLEDGE – PRACTICE TEST 4

1. What you said really <u>intrigues</u> me.
   A. fulfils
   B. appalls
   C. fascinates
   D. subjugates

2. <u>Fatality</u> most nearly means:
   A. death
   B. disinclination
   C. accident
   D. injury

3. Paula has a(n) <u>penchant</u> for collecting antiques.
   A. insinuation
   B. preference
   C. indifference
   D. dissension

4. <u>Implicit</u> most nearly means:
   A. understood
   B. accurate
   C. hidden
   D. unstated

5. His response was <u>incoherent</u>.
   A. unenthusiastic
   B. muffled
   C. incomprehensible
   D. breathless

6. <u>Facilitate</u> most nearly means:
   A. teach
   B. assist
   C. construct
   D. rectify

7. He arrived at the airport <u>incognito</u>.
   A. late
   B. as expected
   C. in disguise
   D. punctually

8. <u>Encompass</u> most nearly means:
   A. involve
   B. anticipate
   C. measure
   D. navigate

9. She has such a <u>strident</u> voice.
   A. kind
   B. loud
   C. sweet
   D. hoarse

10. <u>Verify</u> most nearly means:
    A. conceal
    B. testify
    C. authenticate
    D. demonstrate

11. Knitting and other crafts have experienced a(n) <u>revival</u> recently.
    A. decline
    B. resurgence
    C. awakening
    D. setback

12. Haughty most nearly means:
    A. conceited
    B. breathless
    C. poorly-behaved
    D. ill-mannered

13. The marine displayed great mettle.
    A. skill
    B. courage
    C. adroitness
    D. obedience

14. Jovial most nearly means:
    A. supportive
    B. caring
    C. sincere
    D. cheerful

15. Everyone thought that the accident was ghastly.
    A. unforeseen
    B. serious
    C. hideous
    D. fatal

16. Flounder most nearly means:
    A. go swimming
    B. go fishing
    C. struggle
    D. disbelieve

17. The economy has recently been bolstered by an increase in interest rates.
    A. incited
    B. strengthened
    C. let down
    D. weakened

18. Acuity most nearly means:
    A. precision
    B. illness
    C. ignorance
    D. sensitivity

19. With hindsight, I can see things more clearly now.
    A. with experience
    B. with regret
    C. in remembrance
    D. in retrospect

20. Rigid most nearly means:
    A. stressed
    B. enclosed
    C. unbending
    D. unnerving

21. His father's death precipitated his decision.
    A. hastened
    B. prevented
    C. changed
    D. overcame

22. Lustrous most nearly means:
    A. expensive
    B. shiny
    C. cleansed
    D. shampooed

23. Furor most nearly means:
    A. leader
    B. commander
    C. sorrow
    D. outcry

24. Earnest most nearly means the opposite of:
    A. masculine
    B. athletic
    C. insincere
    D. capable

25. Arcanum most nearly means:
    A. ancient
    B. discrete
    C. dome
    D. mystery

26. Slander most nearly means:
    A. gossip
    B. defame
    C. refute
    D. lie

27. Unblemished most nearly means:
    A. faultless
    B. hygienic
    C. sparking
    D. indefinite

28. Wholesome most nearly means the opposite of:
    A. unhealthful
    B. disingenuous
    C. salutary
    D. salubrious

29. Adept most nearly means:
    A. efficient
    B. awkward
    C. skilled
    D. inept

30. Prosperous most nearly means:
    A. advanced
    B. prolific
    C. unfavorable
    D. successful

31. Salvage most nearly means:
    A. deliver
    B. save
    C. barbaric
    D. uncivilized

32. Valiant most nearly means:
    A. upper-class
    B. extravagant
    C. brave
    D. lavish

33. Pique most nearly means:
    A. amuse
    B. enchant
    C. apply
    D. irritate

34. Upheaval most nearly means:
    A. movement
    B. tumult
    C. launch
    D. hoist

35. Indignant most nearly means:
    A. offended
    B. worried
    C. angry
    D. excited

ASVAB WORD KNOWLEDGE – PRACTICE TEST 5

1. His comments always contain a little bit of sarcasm.
   A. criticism
   B. contempt
   C. bitterness
   D. irony

2. He was lurking at the side of the building.
   A. hiding
   B. waiting
   C. loitering
   D. walking

3. Fraternize most nearly means:
   A. encourage
   B. befriend
   C. support
   D. communicate

4. Disparity most nearly means:
   A. disagreement
   B. disharmony
   C. inequality
   D. impartiality

5. The country's monetary policy is controlled by the government.
   A. interest
   B. investment
   C. foreign
   D. financial

6. The store specializes in various types of apparel.
   A. devices
   B. accessories
   C. clothing
   D. equipment

7. Chimera most nearly means:
   A. fireplace
   B. chimney
   C. setback
   D. illusion

8. Champion most nearly means:
   A. defend
   B. defeat
   C. fight
   D. overthrow

9. She was fettered with many responsibilities.
   A. accompanied
   B. restricted
   C. overjoyed
   D. blessed

10. I have never met a more fickle person.
    A. capricious
    B. fun-loving
    C. determined
    D. reliable

11. Momentous most nearly means:
    A. thought-provoking
    B. short-lived
    C. significant
    D. enormous

12. Perpetual most nearly means the opposite of:
    A. irritating
    B. extensive
    C. continuous
    D. short-lived

13. She is really temperamental in the morning.
    A. grumpy
    B. sleepy
    C. alert
    D. energetic

14. The new law will set a(n) precedent.
    A. system
    B. regulation
    C. exemplar
    D. authority

15. Juvenile most nearly means:
    A. underdeveloped
    B. immature
    C. inexperienced
    D. inexpert

16. Feeble most nearly means:
    A. forgetful
    B. old-age
    C. fake
    D. weak

17. She was commended for her actions.
    A. praised
    B. reported
    C. reprimanded
    D. criticized

18. Ostensibly, he is a nice person.
    A. obviously
    B. seemingly
    C. occasionally
    D. rarely

19. Aloof most nearly means:
    A. lonely
    B. lofty
    C. indifferent
    D. confident

20. Confiscate most nearly means:
    A. claim
    B. seize
    C. inspect
    D. remove

21. We will have to tolerate her behavior.
    A. blame
    B. castigate
    C. welcome
    D. endure

22. They were looking forward to the advent of their boss.
    A. season
    B. celebration
    C. arrival
    D. birth

23. All applicants must undergo a stringent background investigation.
    A. strict
    B. handy
    C. brief
    D. stingy

24. Jeopardy most nearly means:
    A. immunity
    B. exposure
    C. danger
    D. depth

25. Putrid most nearly means:
    A. awful
    B. inedible
    C. smelly
    D. rotten

26. He approaches every task with alacrity.
    A. eagerness
    B. reluctance
    C. reproach
    D. wholesomeness

27. The king abdicated his power.
    A. renewed
    B. relinquished
    C. rejected
    D. reinforced

28. Futile most nearly means:
    A. unnecessary
    B. pointless
    C. fecund
    D. fruitful

29. Inimical most nearly means:
    A. imitated
    B. mocked
    C. adverse
    D. averse

30. Florence Nightingale was undaunted in her work, even in times of crisis.
    A. crucial
    B. decisive
    C. admirable
    D. intrepid

31. The prison officers usually subjugate prisoners who attempt to riot.
    A. discourage
    B. punish
    C. prevent
    D. suppress

32. Reticent most nearly means:
    A. taciturn
    B. humble
    C. ebullient
    D. depressed

33. Unscrupulous most nearly means the opposite of:
    A. frank
    B. honest
    C. corrupt
    D. ruthless

34. Winsome most nearly means:
    A. triumphant
    B. victorious
    C. charming
    D. vanquishing

35. Renovate most nearly means:
    A. restore
    B. demolish
    C. clean up
    D. dispose of

ASVAB WORD KNOWLEDGE – PRACTICE TEST 6

1. The company has been <u>dormant</u> since 2012.
   A. successful
   B. viable
   C. incorporated
   D. inactive

2. She always has the most <u>ingenious</u> ideas.
   A. benevolent
   B. ridiculous
   C. popular
   D. inventive

3. You will be given more information when the ceremony <u>commences</u>.
   A. concludes
   B. begins
   C. continues
   D. culminates

4. <u>Propensity</u> most nearly means:
   A. enthusiasm
   B. interest
   C. proclivity
   D. competence

5. <u>Domineer</u> most nearly means:
   A. dominate
   B. threaten
   C. submit
   D. surrender

6. The governor decided to show <u>clemency</u> to the prisoners.
   A. justice
   B. mercy
   C. peace
   D. hope

7. He said that we have to <u>abridge</u> the document.
   A. shorten
   B. interpret
   C. mail
   D. file

8. <u>Abyss</u> most nearly means:
   A. infection
   B. inflammation
   C. chasm
   D. valley

9. <u>Pugnacious</u> most nearly means:
   A. fearless
   B. tenacious
   C. vigorous
   D. quarrelsome

10. Of all of the volunteers on the campaign, she has been the most <u>stalwart</u>.
    A. strong
    B. loyal
    C. defensive
    D. resilient

11. The high salary <u>enticed</u> him into accepting the job.
    A. tricked
    B. blackmailed
    C. lured
    D. bribed

12. The accountant determined the cumulative amount of the expenses.
    A. total
    B. excessive
    C. yearly
    D. costly

13. Her job is as president of the college is trying.
    A. demanding
    B. interesting
    C. experimental
    D. boring

14. Trite most nearly means:
    A. wasteful
    B. impure
    C. brief
    D. banal

15. Unscathed most nearly means:
    A. healthy
    B. unharmed
    C. impaired
    D. spoiled

16. Abhorrent most nearly means:
    A. relinquished
    B. ceased
    C. detestable
    D. commendable

17. Her story was full of hyperbole.
    A. enchantment
    B. exhilaration
    C. preoccupation
    D. exaggeration

18. He might find it hard to make friends at college because he is so studious.
    A. bookish
    B. selfish
    C. aloof
    D. serious

19. Transpose most nearly means:
    A. note down
    B. exchange
    C. interpose
    D. interject

20. Respite most nearly means:
    A. inhale
    B. breathe
    C. rest
    D. recuperate

21. Suppress most nearly means the opposite of:
    A. subdue
    B. defeat
    C. control
    D. incite

22. Purge most nearly means:
    A. eliminate
    B. escalate
    C. upsurge
    D. filtrate

23. Opaque most nearly means the opposite of:
    A. obscure
    B. cloudy
    C. darkened
    D. transparent

24. Her taste in clothing is very eccentric.
    A. trendy
    B. stylish
    C. unconventional
    D. distinctive

25. Their relationship is full of acrimony.
    A. sarcasm
    B. disharmony
    C. ambiguity
    D. ambivalence

26. Carrying out their strategy involved intricate planning.
    A. complex
    B. lengthy
    C. manageable
    D. cooperative

27. Precinct most nearly means:
    A. station
    B. office
    C. territory
    D. site

28. Remunerate most nearly means:
    A. advance
    B. reclaim
    C. acquire
    D. compensate

29. Satire most nearly means:
    A. mockery
    B. contempt
    C. ill feeling
    D. practical joke

30. Mulct most nearly means:
    A. deceive
    B. defraud
    C. shred
    D. decompose

31. Disclose most nearly means:
    A. publicize
    B. circulate
    C. unfold
    D. uncover

32. Calamity most nearly means:
    A. threat
    B. danger
    C. disaster
    D. disease

33. Artifact most nearly means:
    A. actuality
    B. certainty
    C. antique
    D. relic

34. Dispatch most nearly means:
    A. send out
    B. go forward
    C. state
    D. communicate

35. Paradigm most nearly means:
    A. order
    B. model
    C. summit
    D. culmination

ASVAB WORD KNOWLEDGE – PRACTICE TEST 7

1. The villain robbed the bank, killing two people.
   A. prisoner
   B. robber
   C. murderer
   D. outlaw

2. Wayward most nearly means:
   A. purposeless
   B. pointless
   C. contrary
   D. curved

3. We need to consider the consequences of our actions.
   A. success of
   B. motivations for
   C. reasons for
   D. results of

4. Acquiesce most nearly means:
   A. accept
   B. ignore
   C. assimilate
   D. accommodate

5. Ford is a(n) forerunner in the automotive industry.
   A. enterprise
   B. company
   C. leader
   D. giant

6. Patent most nearly means:
   A. showy
   B. visible
   C. obscure
   D. permitted

7. The vacation that they had planned failed to materialize.
   A. be enjoyable
   B. continue
   C. prevail
   D. happen

8. Lenient most nearly means:
   A. easy-going
   B. lazy
   C. improper
   D. insolent

9. They operate a legitimate business activity.
   A. prosperous
   B. profitable
   C. defunct
   D. lawful

10. Dismal most nearly means:
    A. ill-advised
    B. poorly planned
    C. disastrous
    D. erroneous

11. Gossiping about others can actually be quite pernicious.
    A. extensive
    B. damaging
    C. truthful
    D. exciting

12. This machine has a defect which prevents it from functioning.
    A. fault
    B. safety
    C. problem
    D. protection

13. The house was engulfed in flames.
    A. ablaze in
    B. ignited by
    C. incinerated by
    D. overcome by

14. Façade most nearly means:
    A. deface
    B. apparel
    C. appearance
    D. incognito

15. Propitiate most nearly means:
    A. appease
    B. modify
    C. rain
    D. snow

16. Ephemeral most nearly means:
    A. adorned
    B. bejeweled
    C. enduring
    D. short-lived

17. They used several gimmicks to sell their product.
    A. advertisements
    B. promotions
    C. tricks
    D. discounts

18. I really don't think he should dispense advice to you.
    A. offer
    B. give
    C. exclude
    D. dismiss

19. Advocate most nearly means:
    A. judge
    B. proponent
    C. adversary
    D. arbiter

20. Laud most nearly means:
    A. observe
    B. proclaim
    C. honor
    D. bolster

21. The amount he is paid is a pittance.
    A. insufficient
    B. shameful
    C. permitted
    D. illegal

22. He sat by the lake, contemplating his problems.
    A. reviewing
    B. reliving
    C. trying to forget
    D. thinking about

23. This pipe has been galvanized with a special coating.
    A. treated
    B. covered
    C. fabricated
    D. strengthened

24. Dubious most nearly means:
    A. unfavorable
    B. doubtful
    C. undeniable
    D. pessimistic

25. A(n) noxious gas was used in order to eliminate all of the insects.
    A. invisible
    B. innocuous
    C. toxic
    D. luxurious

26. The troops will debouch at the base of the valley.
    A. emerge
    B. camp
    C. disarm
    D. strategize

27. Parity most nearly means:
    A. verity
    B. equality
    C. combine
    D. establish

28. Accord most nearly means:
    A. antagonist
    B. advocate
    C. resemblance
    D. agreement

29. Bequest most nearly means:
    A. appeal
    B. application
    C. inheritance
    D. grant

30. Perturb most nearly means:
    A. annoy
    B. astound
    C. fascinate
    D. stimulate

31. Reproach most nearly means:
    A. access
    B. criticize
    C. prove
    D. rescind

32. Concatenation most nearly means:
    A. noise
    B. disorder
    C. territory
    D. combination

33. Eulogy most nearly means:
    A. speech
    B. tribute
    C. funeral
    D. remembrance

34. Temporal most nearly means:
    A. spiritual
    B. psychological
    C. earthly
    D. ephemeral

35. Vigilant most nearly means:
    A. watchful
    B. restless
    C. defensive
    D. sleepless

ASVAB WORD KNOWLEDGE – PRACTICE TEST 8

1. He is currently being prosecuted for armed robbery.
   A. suspected of
   B. tried for
   C. committed of
   D. sentenced for

2. Reclusive most nearly means:
   A. gregarious
   B. garrulous
   C. solitary
   D. exceptional

3. Obsequious most nearly means:
   A. decorated
   B. showy
   C. subservient
   D. introverted

4. Anomie most nearly means:
   A. seafood
   B. shellfish
   C. despair
   D. chaos

5. She was usually cynical about other people's motives.
   A. distrustful
   B. sarcastic
   C. reluctant
   D. resisting

6. Extraneous most nearly means:
   A. irreverent
   B. irrelevant
   C. eliminated
   D. obscure

7. Blatant most nearly means:
   A. profuse
   B. vague
   C. flagrant
   D. mysterious

8. Fervid most nearly means:
   A. illuminated
   B. afflicted
   C. nervous
   D. ardent

9. The judge lessened the sentence for the crime due to mitigating circumstances.
   A. extenuating
   B. implicating
   C. incriminating
   D. swindling

10. Defray most nearly means:
    A. tear
    B. bear
    C. exude
    D. intensify

11. Nefarious most nearly means:
    A. foreign
    B. peripheral
    C. wicked
    D. nebulous

12. Liaison most nearly means:
    A. avoidance
    B. clandestine
    C. complication
    D. communication

13. Garrison most nearly means:
    A. fort
    B. barracks
    C. latrine
    D. duty

14. She always seems to have some malady.
    A. complaint
    B. illness
    C. comment
    D. compliment

15. Antecedent most nearly means:
    A. event
    B. precursor
    C. death
    D. consequence

16. Jetty most nearly means:
    A. abandon
    B. overboard
    C. pier
    D. cargo

17. Parking fines are not considered to be serious infringements.
    A. regulations
    B. deterrents
    C. ordinances
    D. offenses

18. Proviso most nearly means:
    A. stipulation
    B. ration
    C. plan
    D. arrangement

19. Turbulent most nearly means:
    A. quiescent
    B. windy
    C. powerful
    D. tumultuous

20. The suspect was exonerated for the crime.
    A. exposed
    B. deliberated
    C. cleared
    D. freed

21. Zest most nearly means:
    A. enthusiasm
    B. strength
    C. courage
    D. ambition

22. Resolute most nearly means:
    A. corrupt
    B. licentious
    C. degenerate
    D. determined

23. Unilateral most nearly means:
    A. approved
    B. accepted
    C. one-sided
    D. universal

24. Vestibule most nearly means:
    A. room
    B. entrance
    C. cloak
    D. coat

25. In the end, my input was incidental.
    A. minor
    B. overlooked
    C. detrimental
    D. significant

26. Servility most nearly means:
    A. hospitality
    B. hostility
    C. abandonment
    D. submissiveness

27. We need to avoid mawkish comments if we are going to remain positive.
    A. defamatory
    B. malicious
    C. maudlin
    D. negative

28. Indispensable most nearly means:
    A. permanent
    B. necessary
    C. stalwart
    D. non-degradable

29. No one could understand the nebulous instructions.
    A. extensive
    B. unclear
    C. verbose
    D. complicated

30. Subterfuge most nearly means:
    A. trickery
    B. artillery
    C. bombardment
    D. vicissitude

31. Pending most nearly means:
    A. low hanging
    B. ventilated
    C. impervious
    D. undecided

32. Obsolete most nearly means:
    A. superfluous
    B. perfunctory
    C. broken
    D. outdated

33. We need to rectify a few items on the report.
    A. change
    B. comment on
    C. correct
    D. clarify

34. Sycophant most nearly means:
    A. musician
    B. flatterer
    C. complainer
    D. superior

35. Vindictive most nearly means:
    A. revengeful
    B. conquering
    C. domineering
    D. malcontent

ANSWERS TO THE EXERCISES

Answers – A:

1) affiliation

2) affable, amiable

3) acrimony, animosity

4) arduous

5) alacrity

6) apposite

7) adversaries

8) abrogated

9) alluded

10) ambiance

Answers – B:

1) boisterous

2) bulwarks

3) breach

4) buoys

5) buffoon

6) bland

7) belittles

8) baffled

9) blandishment

10) brusque

Answers – C:

1) castigated

2) capsized

3) cognizant

4) cursory

5) clandestine

6) collaboration

7) condone

8) capitulated

9) carousing

10) cogent

Answers – D:

1) dense

2) despicable, deplorable

3) diligent

4) dismantled

5) diversified

6) digressed

7) docile

8) dulcet

9) didactic

10) de facto

Answers – E:

1) elusive

2) enervating

3) enterprise, entity

4) exacerbate

5) extenuating

6) entails

7) effigy

8) eldritch

9) embezzling

10) equivocating

Answers – F:

1) facetious

2) flanked

3) fortuitous

4) frivolous

5) fundamental

6) fulsome

7) flourish

8) foiled

9) fiasco

10) fallacious

Answers – G to H:

1) glut

2) heinous

3) guileless

4) grumbles

5) hypocrite

6) hoarse

7) helm

8) hunch

9) garbled

10) garrulous

Answers – I:

1) immaculate

2) implicated, incriminated

3) impertinent, insolent

4) inhabitant

5) impeccable

6) instigated

7) idle

8) implored

9) indefatigable, illustrious, intrepid

10) immutable

Answers – J to L:

1) lassitude, lethargy

2) latent

3) loquacious

4) juvenile, ludic

5) kvetch

6) laconic

7) jargon

8) liabilities

9) licentious

10) jurisdiction

Answers – M to O:

1) obliterated

2) nominated

3) obstinate

4) overabundance

5) mauled

6) magnanimity

7) noxious

8) mandatory

9) ostentatious

10) mitigated

Answers – P:

1) phlegmatic

2) pillaged

3) parsimonious

4) pensive

5) precarious, prostrate

6) preemptive

7) perfidy

8) protracted

9) perceptible

10) poignant

Answers – Q to R:

1) rehabilitation

2) render

3) repast

4) rodents

5) qualms

6) relinquish

7) rejuvenate

8) querulous

9) retrospect

10) reluctant

Answers – S:

1) sedulous

2) sinecure

3) stagnant

4) slipshod

5) slovenly

6) squalor

7) simulate

8) strenuous

9) sanctimonious

10) salvo

Answers – T:

1) testify

2) trying, tedious

3) tenets

4) truncated

5) tantamount

6) tangible

7) tardiness

8) thwarted

9) terse

10) throng

Answers – U to V:

1) vacillated

2) undermined

3) verdict

4) undertaking

5) unconventional

6) venue

7) vicissitudes

8) ultimatum

9) unwavering

10) unsavory, vulgar

Answers – W to Z:

1) wary

2) zealot

3) wither

4) weary, wretched

5) weal

6) zest

7) wry

8) yearned

9) wistful

10) wrath

ANSWERS TO THE PRACTICE TESTS

Test 1:

1) B
2) C
3) A
4) D
5) B
6) D
7) A
8) C
9) B
10) D
11) D
12) A
13) B
14) C
15) D
16) A
17) B
18) C
19) B
20) D
21) A
22) D
23) C
24) B
25) D
26) A
27) C
28) D
29) B
30) A
31) C
32) B
33) D
34) A
35) C

Test 2:

1) C
2) A
3) D
4) D
5) B
6) D
7) A
8) B
9) C
10) D
11) A
12) B
13) D
14) C
15) A
16) A
17) B
18) D
19) C
20) B
21) A
22) D
23) C
24) B
25) A
26) A
27) B
28) C
29) D
30) D
31) D
32) B
33) C
34) C
35) D

Test 3:

1) B
2) C
3) A
4) D
5) D
6) A
7) B
8) C
9) D
10) A
11) B
12) A
13) D
14) B
15) B
16) A
17) C
18) A
19) D
20) B
21) B
22) C
23) C
24) A
25) D
26) B
27) D
28) C
29) A
30) B
31) D
32) A
33) C
34) B
35) D

Test 4:

1) C
2) A
3) B
4) D
5) C
6) B
7) C
8) A
9) D
10) C
11) B
12) A
13) B
14) D
15) C
16) C
17) B
18) A
19) D
20) C
21) A
22) B
23) D
24) C
25) D
26) B
27) A
28) A
29) C
30) D
31) B
32) C
33) D
34) B
35) A

Test 5:

1) D
2) A
3) B
4) C
5) D
6) C
7) D
8) A
9) B
10) A
11) C
12) D
13) A
14) C
15) B
16) D
17) A
18) B
19) C
20) B
21) D
22) C
23) A
24) C
25) D
26) A
27) B
28) B
29) C
30) D
31) D
32) A
33) B
34) C
35) A

Test 6:

1) D
2) D
3) B
4) C
5) A
6) B
7) A
8) C
9) D
10) B
11) C
12) A
13) A
14) D
15) B
16) C
17) D
18) A
19) B
20) C
21) D
22) A
23) D
24) C
25) B
26) A
27) C
28) D
29) A
30) B
31) D
32) C
33) D
34) A
35) B

Test 7:

1) D
2) C
3) D
4) A
5) C
6) B
7) D
8) A
9) D
10) C
11) B
12) A
13) D
14) C
15) A
16) D
17) C
18) B
19) B
20) C
21) A
22) D
23) D
24) B
25) C
26) A
27) B
28) D
29) C
30) A
31) B
32) D
33) B
34) C
35) A

Test 8:

1) B
2) C
3) C
4) D
5) A
6) B
7) C
8) D
9) A
10) B
11) C
12) D
13) A
14) B
15) B
16) C
17) D
18) A
19) D
20) C
21) A
22) D
23) C
24) B
25) A
26) D
27) C
28) B
29) B
30) A
31) D
32) D
33) C
34) B
35) A

APPENDIX 1 – ASVAB AND AFQT TEST INFORMATION

The ASVAB Examination (Armed Services Vocational Aptitude Battery) assesses your skills for a career in the military.

The ASVAB is administered both on the computer and in traditional pencil and paper format. The complete pencil-and-paper ASVAB consists of eight sections, while the complete computer-assisted ASVAB consists of nine sections.

You should enquire at your testing location to see which version of the exam they are offering.

If you are still in high school, you should ask your guidance counselor if the ASVAB exam is going to be offered at your school.

You can also take the ASVAB at a Military Entrance Processing Station (MEPS) or at a Mobile Examination Team Site (METS.)

Your guidance counselor or testing officer can also provide information about how you will receive your score report.

You can retake the ASVAB if you are not satisfied with your score. However, there are restrictions associated with retaking the exam, so it will be to your benefit to be well-prepared for your exam when you first take it.

Your AFQT score for the examination consists of only four of the sections of the ASVAB: Word Knowledge, Paragraph Comprehension, Arithmetic Reasoning, and Mathematics Knowledge.

The AFQT (Armed Forces Qualifying Test) score is the most important score for entrance into the military, and you will need to have a certain AFQT score in order to be eligible to enlist. Your AFQT score is also used to decide what kinds of jobs you will be eligible for in the armed services.

Since your AFQT score is so important, you may want to devote extra attention to studying for the AFQT sections of the exam.

APPENDIX 2 – HOW TO USE THIS PUBLICATION FOR SELF-STUDY

This study guide contains vocabulary like you will see on the word knowledge section of the ASVAB examination.

The vocabulary in the book is divided into alphabetized sections, from A to Z. You should study the vocabulary in each section, paying special attention to how the words are used in the example sentences provided.

For each word in the vocabulary lists of each chapter, you should devote some time to studying the derivative words, which are formed with prefixes or suffixes. This is an important aspect of your exam preparation since you may need to know both the noun and adverb forms for a particular word, for instance. The derivatives are provided after the example sentence for each word.

Also pay attention to the metaphorical uses of the words, which indicate how the words or phrases are used in everyday, informal situations.

For optimal performance on the exam, it is advisable to try to commit the words to memory. We recommend that you do this in two steps.

First of all, try to memorize the meanings of the words by placing a card or piece of paper over the definition at the right, while revealing only the word at the left.

When you have done this a few times, you can then highlight the words that you are finding hard to remember. Alternatively, you can make flash cards for the words that you find more troublesome.

If you decide to make flashcards, it is advisable to put the words from the lists on the front of the card and the definitions and synonyms on the reverse.

You may discover words that are unknown to you in the definitions and synonyms provided in this publication. In that case, you should try to memorize this new vocabulary as well.

Once you have studied each section, you should proceed to the exercises at the end of the chapter. The exercises will provide you with further practice in utilizing the vocabulary naturally in sentences, a skill which is assessed on the exam.

You should then check your answers to the exercises by looking at the answers provided at the end of the book.

When you have finished all of the exercises, you should complete the eight extra practice tests at the end of the book.

Each of the practice tests contains 35 questions, just like the actual ASVAB Word Knowledge Test. You should allow yourself 11 minutes to complete each practice test in order to simulate the actual exam.

APPENDIX 3 – INFORMATION FOR EDUCATORS

If you are an educator, please respect copyright law. This book cannot be photocopied or reproduced electronically for use with students.

In order to use the book in a classroom or tutorial setting, you should purchase a copy of the book for each of your students.

For those interested in purchasing sets of materials for classroom use, please contact us for information on bulk discounts. We may be contacted by filling in the "Contact Us" form at www.examsam.com.

The materials in this publication can be utilized with students in a number of ways. First of all, it is recommended to review each chapter with your students in the classroom.

During this activity, focus on the provided words in the lists, as well as the derivative words given after each definition. You should cover how the words are to be correctly used in sentences, since this skill is tested on the exam.

You can then have a pronunciation activity for some of the lesser-known words in order to help students raise the level of their spoken English.

As an in-class follow-up activity, students can write additional sentences using the words from each chapter. The classroom books can be made available as a guide during this time.

On a subsequent day, a closed-book vocabulary quiz should be given. This will encourage students to attempt to memorize the meanings of the words in the chapter during their private self-study time.

When you have completed all of the chapters with your students, you should then attempt the practice tests at the end of the book. This activity should be timed in order to simulate actual exam conditions, with an eleven-minute time limit for each practice test.